AF609476

WEST BENGAL

A STATE STUDY GUIDE

SUBASHISH BHATTACHARYA

Published by

Hawk Press
4836/24, Ansari Road, Daryaganj
New Delhi – 110 002
Phones: 91-11-23278618, 91-11-43667199
E-mail: thehawkpress@gmail.com
www.thehawkpress.com

Copyright © 2018, *Editor*
ISBN: 978-93-88318-69-3
All rights reserved.

No part of this book may be reproduced, stored in a retrieval system, transmitted or utilised in any form or by any means, electronic, mechanical, photocopying, recording or otherwise, without the prior permission of the copyright owner. Application for such permission should be addressed to the publisher.

Preface

West Bengal is an Indian state, located in Eastern India on the Bay of Bengal. With over 91 million inhabitants (as of 2011), it is India's fourth-most populous state. It has an area of 88,752 km (34,267 sq mi). A part of the ethno-linguistic Bengal region of the Indian subcontinent, it borders Bangladesh in the east, and Nepal and Bhutan in the north. It also borders the Indian states of Odisha, Jharkhand, Bihar, Sikkim, and Assam. The state capital is Kolkata (Calcutta), the seventh-largest city in India. As for geography, West Bengal includes the Darjeeling Himalayan hill region, the Ganges delta, the Rarh region, and the coastal Sundarbans. The main ethnic group are the Bengalis, with Bengali Hindus forming the demographic majority.

From the 13th century onward, the region was ruled by several sultans, powerful Hindu states, and Baro-Bhuyan landlords, until the beginning of British rule in the 18th century. The British East India Company cemented their hold on the region following the Battle of Plassey in 1757, and Calcutta served for many years as the capital of British India. The early and prolonged exposure to British administration resulted in an expansion of Western education, culminating in developments in science, institutional education, and social reforms in the region, including what became known as the Bengali Renaissance. A hotbed of the Indian independence movement through the early 20th century, Bengal was divided during India's independence in 1947 along religious lines into two separate entities: West Bengal, a state of India, and East Bengal, a province of Pakistan which later became independent Bangladesh. Between 1977 and 2011 the state was administered by the world's longest elected Communist government.

Geography of West Bengal is full of variety. It consists of high peaks of Himalaya in the northern extremes to coastal regions down south, with regions like plateu, Ganges delta etc. intervening in between. It may be interesting to note that West Bengal is only state in India where Himalayas are in the north and Sea is at the south, with both plaines and plateau are covering the remaining region.

The economy of West Bengal is the sixth-largest state economy in India with 10.49 lakh crore (US$150 billion) in gross domestic product and a per capita GDP of 108,000 (US$1,500). The state's cultural heritage, besides varied folk traditions, includes authors in literature, such as Nobel laureate Rabindranath Tagore. Kolkata is known as the "cultural capital of India". West Bengal is also known for its enthusiasm for the sport of association football, as well as cricket.

In August 2016 the West Bengal Legislative Assembly passed another resolution to change the name of West Bengal to "Bangla" in Hindi, "Bengal" in English, and "Bangla" in Bengali. Despite the Trinamool Congress government's efforts to forge a consensus on the name change resolution, the Indian National Congress, the Left Front, and the Bharatiya Janata Party opposed the resolution. However, the central government has turned down the proposal stating that the state should have one single name for all languages instead of three and also the name should not be the same as that of any other territory (pointing out that the name 'Bangla' may create confusion with neighboring Bangladesh).

This is a reference book. All the matter is just compiled and edited in nature, taken from the various sources which are in public domain.

The book will be highly useful for students, teachers and all those concerned.

—*Editor*

ABOUT THE BOOK

West Bengal is an Indian state, located in Eastern India on the Bay of Bengal. With over 91 million inhabitants (as of 2011), it is India's fourth-most populous state. It has an area of 88,752 km (34,267 sq mi). A part of the ethno-linguistic Bengal region of the Indian subcontinent, it borders Bangladesh in the east, and Nepal and Bhutan in the north. The area's early history featured a succession of Indian empires, internal squabbling, and a tussle between Hinduism and Buddhism for dominance. From the 13th century onward, the region was ruled by several sultans, powerful Hindu states, and Baro-Bhuyan landlords, until the beginning of British rule in the 18th century. The British East India Company cemented their hold on the region following the Battle of Plassey in 1757, and Calcutta served for many years as the capital of British India. The early and prolonged exposure to British administration resulted in an expansion of Western education, culminating in developments in science, institutional education, and social reforms in the region, including what became known as the Bengali Renaissance. A hotbed of the Indian independence movement through the early 20th century, Bengal was divided during India's independence in 1947 along religious lines into two separate entities: West Bengal, a state of India, and East Bengal, a province of Pakistan which later became independent Bangladesh. Between 1977 and 2011 the state was administered by the world's longest elected Communist government. The book will be highly useful for students, teachers and all those concerned.

Contents

1

State at a Glance

West Bengal is an Indian state, located in Eastern India on the Bay of Bengal. With over 91 million inhabitants (as of 2011), it is India's fourth-most populous state. It has an area of 88,752 km (34,267 sq mi). A part of the ethno-linguistic Bengal region of the Indian subcontinent, it borders Bangladesh in the east, and Nepal and Bhutan in the north. It also borders the Indian states of Odisha, Jharkhand, Bihar, Sikkim, and Assam. The state capital is Kolkata (Calcutta), the seventh-largest city in India. As for geography, West Bengal includes the Darjeeling Himalayan hill region, the Ganges delta, the Rarh region, and the coastal Sundarbans. The main ethnic group are the Bengalis, with Bengali Hindus forming the demographic majority.

The area's early history featured a succession of Indian empires, internal squabbling, and a tussle between Hinduism and Buddhism for dominance. Ancient Bengal was the site of several major Janapadas (kingdoms), while the earliest cities date back to the Vedic period. The region was part of several ancient pan-Indian empires, including the Mauryans and Guptas. It was also a bastion of regional kingdoms. The citadel of Gauda served as the capital of the Gauda Kingdom, the Buddhist Pala Empire(eighth to 11th century) and Hindu Sena Empire (11th–12th century). From the 13th century onward, the region was ruled by several sultans, powerful Hindu states, and Baro-Bhuyan landlords, until the beginning of British rule in the 18th century. The British East India Company cemented their hold on the region following the Battle of Plassey in 1757, and Calcutta served for many years as the capital of British India.

The early and prolonged exposure to British administration resulted in an expansion of Western education, culminating in developments in science, institutional education, and social reforms in the region, including what became known as the Bengali Renaissance. A hotbed of the Indian independence movement through the early 20th century, Bengal was divided during India's independence in 1947 along religious lines into two separate entities: West Bengal, a state of India, and East Bengal, a province of Pakistan which later became independent Bangladesh. Between 1977 and 2011 the state was administered by the world's longest elected Communist government.

The economy of West Bengal is the sixth-largest state economy in India with 10.49 lakh crore (US$150 billion) in gross domestic product and a per capita GDP of 108,000 (US$1,500). The state's cultural heritage, besides varied folk traditions, includes authors in literature, such as Nobel laureate Rabindranath Tagore. Kolkata is known as the "cultural capital of India". West Bengal is also known for its enthusiasm for the sport of association football, as well as cricket.

ETYMOLOGY

The origin of the name Bengal (*Bangla* and *Bongo* in Bengali) is unknown. One theory suggests that the word derives from "Bang", a Dravidian tribe that settled the region around 1000 BCE. The Bengali word *Bongo* might have been derived from the ancient kingdom of *Vanga* (or *Banga*). Although some early Sanskrit literature mentions the name *Vanga*, the region's early history is obscure.

At the end of British rule over the Indian subcontinent, the Bengal region was partitioned in 1947 along religious lines into east and west. The eastern part came to be known be as East

Pakistan, the eastern wing of newly born Pakistan and the western part came to be known as West Bengal, which continued as an Indian state.

In 2011 the Government of West Bengal proposed a change in the official name of the state to *PaschimBanga* (Bengali: *Pôshchimbônggô*). This is the native name of the state, literally meaning western Bengal in the native Bengali language. In August 2016 the West Bengal Legislative Assembly passed another resolution to change the name of West Bengal to "Bangla" in Hindi, "Bengal" in English, and "Bangla" in Bengali. Despite the Trinamool Congress government's efforts to forge a consensus on the name change resolution, the Indian National Congress, the Left Front, and the Bharatiya Janata Party opposed the resolution. However, the central government has turned down the proposal stating that the state should have one single name for all languages instead of three and also the name should not be the same as that of any other territory (pointing out that the name 'Bangla' may create confusion with neighboring Bangladesh).

HISTORY

Ancient and classical period

Coin of the King Shashanka, who created the first separate political entity in Bengal, called the Gauda Kingdom.

Stone Age tools dating back 20,000 years have been excavated in the state, showing human occupation 8,000 years earlier than scholars had earlier thought. The region was a part of the Vanga Kingdom, according to the Indian epic *Mahabharata*.Several

Vedic realms were present in the Bengal region, including Vanga, Rarh, Pundravardhana, and the Suhma Kingdom. One of the earliest foreign references to Bengal is a mention by the Ancient Greeks around 100 BCE of a land named Gangaridai, which was located at the mouths of the Ganges. Bengal had overseas trade relations with Suvarnabhumi (Burma, Lower Thailand, the Lower Malay Peninsula, and Sumatra). According to the Sri Lankan chronicle *Mahavamsa,* Prince Vijaya (c.543 – c.505 BCE), a Vanga Kingdomprince, conquered Lanka (modern-day Sri Lanka) and gave the name Sinhala Kingdom to the country.

The kingdom of Magadha was formed in the 7th century BCE, consisting of the regions now comprising Bihar and Bengal. It was one of the four main kingdoms of India at the time of the lives of Mahavira, founder of Jainism, and Gautama Buddha, founder of Buddhism. It consisted of several janapadas, or kingdoms. Under Ashoka, the Maurya Empire of Magadha in the 3rd century BCE extended over nearly all of South Asia, including Afghanistan and parts of Balochistan. From the 3rd to the 6th centuries CE, the kingdom of Magadha served as the seat of the Gupta Empire.

Two kingdoms – Vanga or Samatata, and Gauda – are mentioned in some texts to have appeared after the end of the Gupta Empire although details of their ascendancy are uncertain. The first recorded independent king of Bengal was Shashanka, who reigned in the early 7th century. Shashanka is often recorded in Buddhist annals as an intolerant Hindu ruler who is noted for his persecution of the Buddhists. Shashanka murdered Rajyavardhana, the Buddhist king of Thanesar, and is noted for destroying the Bodhi tree at Bodhgaya, and replacing Buddha statues with Shiva lingams. After a period of anarchy, the Pala dynasty ruled the region for four hundred years starting in the 8th century. It was followed by a shorter reign of the Hindu Sena dynasty.

Some areas of Bengal were invaded by Rajendra Chola I of the Chola dynasty between 1021 and 1023. Islam made its first appearance in Bengal during the 12th century when Sufi missionaries arrived. Later, occasional Muslim raiders reinforced the process of conversion by building mosques, madrasas, and khanqahs. Between 1202 and 1206 Muhammad bin Bakhtiyar Khilji, a military commander from the Delhi Sultanate, overran Bihar and Bengal as far east as Rangpur, Bogra, and the Brahmaputra River. Although he failed to bring Bengal under his control, the expedition defeated Lakshman Sen, whose two sons moved to a place then called Vikramapur (present-day Munshiganj District), where their diminished dominion lasted until the late 13th century.

Medieval and early modern periods

Firoz Minar at Gau□a was built during the Bengal Sultanate.

Subsequent Muslim conquests helped spread Islam throughout the region. The region was ruled by dynasties of the Bengal Sultanate and feudal lords under the Delhi Sultanate for the next few hundred years. The Bengal Sultanate was interrupted for a period of twenty years by a Hindu uprising under Raja Ganesha. In the 16th century, Mughal general Islam Khan conquered Bengal. Administration by governors appointed by the court of the Mughal Empire gave way to semi-independence under the

Nawabs of Murshidabad, who nominally respected the sovereignty of the Mughals in Delhi. Several independent Hindu states were established in Bengal during the Mughal period, including those of Pratapaditya of Jessore District and Raja Sitaram Ray of Bardhaman. The Koch dynasty in northern Bengal flourished during the 16th and 17th centuries; it weathered the Mughals and survived until the advent of the British colonial era.

Colonial period

Ram Mohan Roy is regarded as the "Father of the Bengali Renaissance".

Several European traders reached this area late in the 15th century. The British East India Companydefeated Siraj ud-Daulah, the last independent Nawab, in the Battle of Plassey in 1757. The company gained the right to collect revenue in Bengal subah (province) in 1765 with the signing of the treaty between the East India company and the Mughal emperor following the Battle of Buxar in 1764. The Bengal Presidency was established in 1765; it later incorporated all British-controlled territory north of the

Central Provinces (now Madhya Pradesh), from the mouths of the Ganges and the Brahmaputra to the Himalayas and the Punjab. The Bengal famine of 1770 claimed millions of lives due to tax policies enacted by the British company. Calcutta, the headquarters of the East India company, was named in 1773 as the capital of British-held territories in India. The failed Indian rebellion of 1857 started near Calcutta and resulted in a transfer of authority to the British Crown, administered by the Viceroy of India.

The Bengal Renaissance and the Brahmo Samaj socio-cultural reform movements significantly influenced the cultural and economic life of Bengal. Between 1905 and 1911 an abortive attempt was made to divide the province of Bengal into two zones. Bengal suffered from the Great Bengal famine in 1943, which claimed 3 million lives during World War II. Bengalis played a major role in the Indian independence movement, in which revolutionary groups such as *Anushilan Samiti* and *Jugantar* were dominant. Armed attempts against the British Raj from Bengal reached a climax when news of Subhas Chandra Bose leading the Indian National Army against the British reached Bengal. The Indian National Army was subsequently routed by the British.

Indian independence and afterwards

When India gained independence in 1947, Bengal was partitioned along religious lines. The western part went to the Dominion of India (and was named West Bengal), while the eastern part went to the Dominion of Pakistan as a province called East Bengal (later renamed East Pakistan in 1956). The latter became the independent nation of Bangladesh in 1971. In 1950 the Princely State of Cooch Behar merged with West Bengal. In 1955 the former French enclave of Chandannagar, which had passed into Indian control after 1950, was integrated into West Bengal; portions of Bihar were also subsequently merged with West Bengal. Both West and East Bengal experienced large influxes of refugees during and after partition in 1947.

Refugee resettlement and related issues continued to play a significant role in the politics and socio-economic condition of the state.

The Darjeeling Himalayan Railwaywas designated a UNESCO World Heritage Site in 1999.

During the 1970s and 1980s, severe power shortages, strikes, and a violent Naxalite movement damaged much of the state's infrastructure, leading to a period of economic stagnation. The Bangladesh Liberation War of 1971 resulted in the influx of millions of refugees to West Bengal, causing significant strains on its infrastructure. The 1974 smallpox epidemic killed thousands. West Bengal politics underwent a major change when the Left Front won the 1977 assembly election, defeating the incumbent Indian National Congress. The Left Front, led by the Communist Party of India (Marxist), governed the state for the next three decades.

The state's economic recovery gathered momentum after economic liberalisations were introduced in the mid-1990s by the central government. This was aided by the advent of information technology and IT-enabled services. Starting in the mid-2000s, armed activists conducted minor terrorist attacks in some parts of the state while clashes with the administration took place at several controversial locations over the issue of industrial land acquisition, which became a decisive reason behind the defeat of the ruling Left Front government in the 2011 assembly election. Although the economy was severely damaged during the unrest in the 1970s, the state has managed to revive its economy, steadily throughout the years. The state has shown improvement regarding bandhs(strikes) and educational infrastructure. Significant strides have been made in reducing unemployment. Though the state suffers from substandard healthcare services, a lack of socio-economic development, poor infrastructure, unemployment, and civil violence.

MEDIA

In 2005 West Bengal had 505 published newspapers, of which 389 were in Bengali. *Ananda Bazar Patrika*, published from Kolkata with 1,277,801 daily copies, has the largest circulation for a single-edition, regional language newspaper in India. Other major Bengali newspapers are *Bartaman*, *Sangbad Pratidin*, *Aajkaal*, *Jago Bangla*, *Uttarbanga Sambad*, and *Ganashakti*.

Major English language newspapers include *The Telegraph*, *The Times of India*, *Hindustan Times*, *The Hindu*, *The Statesman*, *The Indian Express*, and *Asian Age*. Some prominent financial dailies such as *The Economic Times*, *Financial Express*, *Business Line*, and *Business Standard* are widely circulated. Vernacular newspapers such as those in Hindi, Nepali, Gujarati, Odia, Urdu, and Punjabi are also read by a select readership.

Doordarshan is the state-owned television broadcaster. Multi system operators provide a mix of Bengali, Nepali, Hindi, English, and international channels via cable. Bengali 24-hour television news channels include ABP Ananda, Tara Newz, Kolkata TV, News Time, 24 Ghanta, Mahuaa Khobor, CTVN Plus, Channel 10, and R Plus. All India Radio is a public radio station. Private FM stations are available only in cities like Kolkata, Siliguri, and Asansol. Vodafone, Airtel, BSNL, Jio, Reliance Communications, Uninor, Aircel, MTS India, Idea Cellular, and Tata DoCoMo are available cellular phone providers. Broadband internet is available in select towns and cities and is provided by the state-run BSNL and by other private companies. Dial-up access is provided throughout the state by BSNL and other providers.

SPORTS

Salt Lake Stadium / Vivekananda Yuva Bharati Krirangan, Kolkata

Cricket and association football are popular sports in the state. West Bengal, unlike most other states of India, is noted for its passion and patronage of football. Kolkata is one of the major centres for football in India and houses top national clubs such as Mohun Bagan Athletic Club, East Bengal Club and Mohammedan Sporting Club.

West Bengal has several large stadiums. Eden Gardens was one of only two 100,000-seat cricket stadiums in the world; renovation before 2011 Cricket World Cup reduced the capacity to 66,000. The stadium is the home to various cricket teams such as the Kolkata Knight Riders, the Bengal cricket team, and the East Zone. The 1987 Cricket World Cup final was hosted in Eden Gardens. Calcutta Cricket and Football Club is the second-oldest cricket club in the world.

Salt Lake Stadium / Vivekananda Yuba Bharati Krirangan (VYBK), is a multipurpose stadium in Kolkata, with a current capacity of 85,000. It is the largest stadium in India by seating capacity. Before its renovation in 2011, it was the second largest football stadium in the world, having a seating capacity of 120,000. It has hosted many national and international sporting events like SAF Games of 1987 and the 2011 FIFA friendly football match between Argentina and Venezuela featuring Lionel Messi. In 2008 Legendary German Goalkeeper, Oliver Kahn played his last farewell match on this ground. The stadium hosted the final match of the 2017 FIFA U-17 World Cup.

Notable sports persons from West Bengal include former Indian national cricket captain Sourav Ganguly, Pankaj Roy, Olympic tennis bronze medallist Leander Paes, and chess grand master Dibyendu Barua.

Panoramic View of the Eden Gardens Stadium during IPL 2008

BENGALI PEOPLE

The Bengali people are the ethnic community from Bengal (divided between India and Bangladesh) on the Indian subcontinent with a history dating back four millennia. They speak Bengali, a language of the eastern Indo-Aryan branch of the Indo-European languages. In their native language, they are referred to as *Bangali*. They are Indo-Aryans closely related to the Oriya, Assamese, Biharis, and other East Indians, as well as the Munda, Proto-Australoid, Tibeto-Burman, Austro-Asiatic and Dravidian peoples. As a result, Bengalis are a heterogeneous and considerably diverse ethnic group. They are mostly concentrated in Bangladesh and in the state of West Bengal in India. There are also a number of Bengali communities scattered in New Delhi and several other states of India, such as Assam, Jharkhand, Bihar, Maharastra, Karnataka, Andhra Pradesh, Madhya Pradesh, Uttar Pradesh, Orissa, and the North-East Indian states, as well as in other countries such as Pakistan, the Middle East, United Kingdom and United States.

ADIVASI

Adivasis, literally "original inhabitants", or tribal people comprise a substantial indigenous minority of the population of India. Indian tribals are also called Atavika (forest dwellers, in Sanskrit texts), Vanvasis or Girijans (hill people, *e.g.* by Mahatma Gandhi).

Tribal peoples are particularly numerous in the Indian states of Orissa, Madhya Pradesh, Chattisgarh, Rajasthan, Gujarat, Maharashtra, Andhra Pradesh, Bihar, Jharkhand, West Bengal and in extreme northeastern states such as Mizoram. Officially recognized by the Indian government as "Scheduled Tribes" in the Fifth Schedule of the Constitution of India, they are often grouped together with scheduled castes in the category "Scheduled Castes and Tribes", which is eligible for certain affirmative action measures. During the 19th century, substantial numbers converted to Christianity.

Many smaller tribal groups are quite sensitive to ecological degradation caused by modernization. Both commercial forestry and intensive agriculture have proved destructive to the forests that had endured swidden agriculture for many centuries. See List of Scheduled Tribes in India for a full list of peoples recognized as tribal under the Constitution of India. There were several Adivasis in the Indian independence movement including Khajya Naik, Bhima Naik, Jantya Bhil and Rehma Vasave.

HISTORY

West Bengal pronunciation is a state in eastern India. With Bangladesh, which lies on its eastern border, the state forms the ethno-linguistic region of Bengal. To its northeast lie the states of Assam and Sikkim and the country Bhutan, and to its southwest, the state of Orissa. To the west it borders the state of Jharkhand and Bihar, and to the northwest, Nepal.

The region that is now West Bengal was a part of a number of empires and kingdoms during the past two millennia. The British East India Company cemented their hold on the region following the Battle of Plassey in 1757 CE, and the city of Kolkata, then Kolkata, served for many years as the capital of British India. A hotbed of the Indian independence movement through the early 20th century, Bengal was divided in 1947 into two separate entities, West Bengal - a state of India, and East Pakistan belonging to the new nation of Pakistan.

Following India's independence in 1947, West Bengal's economic and political theatres were dominated for many decades by intellectual Marxism, Naxalite movements and trade unionism. From late 1990s, economic rejuvenation led to a spurt in the state's economic and industrial growth. An agriculture-dependent state, West Bengal occupies only 2.7% of the India's land area, though it supports over 7.8% of Indian population, and is the most densely populated state in India. West Bengal has been ruled by the CPI(M)-led Left Front for three decades, making it the world's longest-running democratically-elected communist government. Many notable poets, writers, artists and performers are native to West Bengal.

Remnants of civilisation in the greater Bengal region date back 4,000 years, when the region was settled by Dravidian, Tibeto-Burman and Austro-Asiatic peoples. The exact origin of the word *Bangla* or Bengal is unknown, though it is believed to be derived from the Dravidian-speaking tribe *Bang* that settled in the area around the year 1000 BC. After the arrival of Indo-Aryans, the kingdom of Magadha was formed in 7th century BC, consisting of the Bihar and Bengal regions.

It was one of the four main kingdoms of India at the time of Buddha and consisted of several *Janapadas*. Under the Maurya dynasty founded by Chandragupta Maurya, the Magadha Empire extended over nearly all of South Asia, including parts of Persia and Afghanistan under Ashoka the Great in the 3rd century BC. One of the earliest foreign references to Bengal is the mention of a land named Gangaridai by the Greeks around 100 BC. The word is speculated to have come from *Gangahrd* (Land with the Ganges in its heart) in reference to an area in Bengal.

From the 3rd to the 6th centuries CE, the kingdom of Magadha served as the seat of the Gupta Empire. The first recorded independent king of Bengal was Shashanka, reigning around early 7th century. After a period of anarchy, the Buddhist Pala dynasty ruled the region for four hundred years, followed by a shorter reign of the Hindu Sena dynasty. Islam was introduced to Bengal in the twelfth century by Sufi missionaries. Subsequent Muslim conquests helped spread Islam throughout the region. Bakhtiar Khilji, a Turkic general of the Slave dynasty of Delhi Sultanate, defeated Lakshman Sen of the Sena dynasty and conquered large parts of Bengal. Consequently, the region was ruled by dynasties of sultans and feudal lords under the Delhi Sultanate for the next few hundred years. In the sixteenth century, Mughal general Islam Khan conquered Bengal. However, administration by governors appointed by the court of the Mughal Empire gave way to semi-independence of the area under the Nawabs of Murshidabad, who nominally respected the sovereignty of the Mughals in Delhi.

European traders arrived late in the fifteenth century. Their influence grew until the British East India Company gained taxation rights in Bengal *subah*, or province, following the Battle of Plassey in 1757, when Siraj-ud-Daulah, the last independent Nawab, was defeated by the British. The Bengal

Presidency was established by 1765, eventually including all British territories north of the Central Provinces (now Madhya Pradesh), from the mouths of the Ganges and the Brahmaputra to the Himalayas and the Punjab.

The Bengal famine of 1770 claimed millions of lives. Kolkata was named the capital of British India in 1772. The Bengal Renaissance and Brahmo Samaj socio-cultural reform movements had great impact on the cultural and economic life of Bengal. The failed Indian rebellion of 1857 started near Kolkata and resulted in transfer of authority to the British Crown, administered by the Viceroy of India. Between 1905 and 1911, an abortive attempt was made to divide the province of Bengal into two zones. Bengal suffered from the Great Bengal famine in 1943 that claimed 3 million lives.

Bengal played a major role in the Indian independence movement, in which revolutionary groups such as Anushilan Samiti and Jugantar were dominant. Armed attempts against the British Raj from Bengal reached a climax when Subhash Chandra Bose led the Indian National Army against the British. When India gained independence in 1947, Bengal was partitioned along religious lines. The western part went to India (and was named West Bengal) while the eastern part joined Pakistan as a province called East Bengal (later renamed East Pakistan, giving rise to Bangladesh in 1971). In 1955, the former French enclave of Chandannagar, which had passed into Indian control after 1950, was integrated into West Bengal; portions of Bihar were subsequently merged with West Bengal.

During the 1960s and 1970s, severe power shortages, strikes and a violent Marxist-Naxalite movement damaged much of the state's infrastructure, leading to a period of economic stagnation. The Bangladesh Liberation War of 1971 resulted in the influx of millions of refugees to West Bengal, causing significant strains on its infrastructure. West Bengal politics underwent a major change when the Left Front won the 1977 assembly election, defeating the incumbent Indian National Congress. The Left Front, led by CPI(M) has governed for the last three decades.

The state's economic recovery gathered momentum after economic reforms in India were introduced in the mid-1990s by the central government, aided by election of a new reformist Chief Minister in 2000. As of 2007, armed Maoist activists have been organising minor terrorist attacks in some parts of the state, while clashes with the administration are taking place at several sensitive places on the issue of industrial land acquisition.

BENGAL RENAISSANCE

The Bengal Renaissance refers to a social reform movement during the nineteenth and early twentieth centuries in the region of Bengal in undivided India during the period of British rule. The Bengal renaissance can be said to have started with Raja Ram Mohan Roy (1775-1833) and ended with Rabindranath Tagore (1861-1941), although there have been many stalwarts thereafter embodying particular aspects of the unique intellectual and creative output. Nineteenth century Bengal was a unique blend of religious and social reformers, scholars, literary giants, journalists, patriotic orators and scientists, all merging to form the image of a renaissance, and marked the transition from the 'medieval' to the 'modern'.

Background: During this period, Bengal witnessed an intellectual awakening that is in some way similar to the Renaissance in Europe during the 16th century, although Europeans of that age were not confronted with the challenge and influence of alien colonialism.

This movement questioned existing orthodoxies, particularly with respect to women, marriage, the dowry system, the caste system, and religion. One of the earliest social movements that emerged during this time was the Young Bengal movement, that espoused rationalism and atheism as the common denominators of civil conduct among upper caste educated Hindus.

The parallel socio-religious movement, the Brahmo Samaj, developed during this time period and counted many of the leaders of the Bengal Renaissance among its followers. In the earlier years the Brahmo Samaj, like the rest of society, could not however, conceptualize, in that feudal-colonial era, a free India as it was influenced by the European Enlightenment (and its bearers in India, the British Raj) although it traced its intellectual roots to the Upanishads.

Their version of Hinduism, or rather Universal Religion (similar to that of Ramakrishna), although devoid of social evils like sati, purdah and polygamy that had crept within Hinduism during the Islamic rule, was ultimately a rigid impersonal monotheistic faith, which actually was quite distinct from the pluralistic and multifaceted nature of the Hindu religion. Future leaders like Keshub Chunder Sen were as much devotees of Christ, as they were of Brahma, Krishna or the Buddha. It has been argued by some scholars that the Brahmo Samaj movement never gained the support of the masses and remained restricted to the elite, although Hindu society has accepted most of the social reform programmes of the Brahmo Samaj. It must also be acknowledged that many of the later Brahmos were also leaders of the freedom movement.

The renaissance period after the Indian Rebellion of 1857 saw a magnificent outburst of Bengali literature. While Ram Mohan Roy and Iswar Chandra Vidyasagar were the pioneers, others like Bankim Chandra Chatterjee widened it and built upon it. The first significant nationalist detour to the Bengal Renaissance was given by the brilliant writings of Bankim Chandra Chatterjee.

Later, Ramakrishna Paramhansa, a great saint of Bengal, is thought to have realized the mystical truth of all religions, and to have reconciled the conflicting Hindu sects ranging from Shakta tantra, Advaita Vedanta and Vaishnavism, as well as other religions like Christianity and Islam. The Vedanta movement prospered principally through his disciple and sage, Swami Vivekananda who on his return from the highly successful Parliament of the World's Religions in Chicago in 1893 and subsequent lecture tour in America, became a revered national idol.

He urged Indians to break free from the shackles of colonialism, past and present and reaffirmed service to mankind as the highest truth of the Hindu Vedantic religion. "Service to mankind is service to god" was his motto. He was the first Indian to conceptualize an absolutely free, prosperous and strong India, which while appreciative of its rich cultural past would be vibrant enough to walk confidently into the future. Ramakrishna Mission, the great organization founded by Swami Vivekananda, was totally non-political in nature.

The Tagore family, including Rabindranath Tagore were leaders of this period and had a particular interest in educational reform. Their contribution to the Bengal Renaissance was multi-faceted. Indeed, Tagore's 1901 Bengali novella, *Nastanirh* was written as a critique of men who professed to follow the ideals of the Renaissance, but failed to do so within their own families. That is only one example but the contribution of the family is enormous.

Comparison with European Renaissance

The word "renaissance" in European history meant "rebirth" and was used in the context of the revival of the Graeco-Roman learning in the fifteenth and sixteenth centuries after the long winter of the dark medieval period. A serious comparison was started by the dramatis personae of the Bengal renaissance like Keshub Chunder Sen, Bipin Chandra Pal and M. N. Roy. For about a century, Bengal's conscious awareness and the changing modern world was more developed and ahead of that of rest of India.

The role played by Bengal in the modern awakening of India is thus comparable to the position occupied by Italy in the European renaissance. Very much like the Italian renaissance, it was not a mass movement but restricted to the upper classes. Though the Bengal Renaissance was the "culmination of the process of emergence of the cultural characteristics of the Bengali people that had started in the age of Hussein Shah, it remained predominantly Hindu and only partially Muslim." There were isolated examples of Muslim intellectuals like Saiyed Amir Ali and Mosharraf Hussain.

Some scholars in Bangladesh, now hold Bengal Renaissance in a different light. As Professor Muin-ud-Din Ahmad Khan of the department of Islamic History and Culture of Chittagong University, observes.

During nineteenth century AD., Bengal produced a galaxy of reform movements among the Hindus as well Muslims... the Islamic reform movements such as Faraizi, Tariquah-i-Muhhamadiyah, and Taaiyni and Ahl-i-Hadith, occupied a conspicuous position amongst them. These Islamic movements were revivalist in character... these Islamic movements were born of the circumstances, which had also given birth to the contemporary Hindu reform movements such as Brahmo Samaj and Arya Samaj, which thrived in Bengal side by side with them... Raja Ram Mohan Roy's movement is generally regarded as 'Renaissance movement'.

It is called by some as 'Hindu Renaissance' and by others as 'Bengali Renaissance' movement. It should nevertheless be observed that compared with the European 'Renaissance model', it was a Renaissance with a difference, especially, deeply inlaid by a revivalist make-up of pristine Hindu or Aryan religious spirit...Raja Ram Mohan Roy's Renaissance aimed at resuscitating the pristine Aryan spirit, 'Unitarianism of God', with the help of modern Western rationalist spirit.

PARTITION OF BENGAL (1905)

The Partition of Bengal in 1905, was made on 16 October by then Viceroy of India, Lord Curzon. Due to the high level of political unrest generated by the partition, the eastern and western parts of Bengal were reunited in 1912.

Origin: The province of Bengal had an area of 189,000 sq. miles and a population of 78.5 million. Eastern Bengal was almost isolated from the western part by geography and poor communications. In 1836, the upper provinces were placed under a lieutenant governor, and in 1854 the Governor-General-

In-Council was relieved of the direct administration of Bengal. In 1874 Assam, including Sylhet, was severed from Bengal to form a Chief-Commissionership, and the Lushai Hills were added to it in 1898.

Partition: Partitioning Bengal was first considered in 1903. There were also additional proposals to separate Chittagong and the districts of Dhaka and Mymensingh from Bengal and attaching them to the province of Assam. Similarly incorporating Chhota Nagpur with the central provinces.

The government officially published the idea in January 1904, and in February, Lord Curzon made an official tour to eastern districts of Bengal to assess public opinion on the partition. He consulted with leading personalities and delivered speeches at Dhaka, Chittagong and Mymensingh explaining the government's stand on partition.

The new province would consist of the state of Hill Tripura, the Divisions of Chittagong, Dhaka and Rajshahi (excluding Darjeeling) and the district of Malda incorporated with Assam province. Bengal was to surrender not only these large eastern territories but also to cede to the Central Provinces the five Hindi-speaking states. On the western side it was offered Sambalpur and five minor Oriya-speaking states from the Central Provinces. Bengal would be left with an area of 141,580 sq. miles and population of 54 million, of which 42 million would be Hindus and 9 million Muslims.

The new province was named Eastern Bengal and Assam with Dhaka as its capital and subsidiary headquarters at Chittagong. Its area would be 106,540 sq. miles with a population of 31 million, where 18 million would be Muslims and 12 million Hindus. Administration would consist of a Legislative Council, a Board of Revenue of two members, and the jurisdiction of the Kolkata High Court would be left undisturbed. The government pointed out that Eastern Bengal and Assam would have a clearly demarcated western boundary and well defined geographical, ethnological, linguistic and social characteristics. The government of India promulgated their final decision in a resolution dated July 19, 1905 and the partition of Bengal was effected on October 16 of same year.

This created a huge political crisis. The Muslims in East Bengal had the impression that a separate region would give them more opportunity for education, employment etc. However, the partition was not liked by the people in West Bengal and a huge amount of nationalist literature was created there during this period. Opposition by Indian National Congress was led by Sir Henry Cotton who had been Chief Commissioner of Assam, but Curzon was not to be moved. Later, Cotton, now Liberal MP for Nottingham East coordinated the successful campaign to oust the first lieutenant-governor of East Bengal, Sir Bampfylde Fuller. In 1906, Rabindranath Tagore wrote Amar Shonar Bangla as a rallying cry for proponents of annulment of Partition, which, much later, in 1972, became the national anthem of Bangladesh.

Due to these political protests, the two parts of Bengal were reunited in 1912. A new partition which divided the province on linguistic, rather than religious, grounds followed, with the Hindi, Oriya and Assamese areas separated to form separate administrative units. The administrative capital of British India was moved from Kolkata to New Delhi as well.

However, conflict between Muslims and Hindus resulted in new laws having to be introduced so as to satisfy the political needs of both groups.

2

Culture and Society

CULTURE

The Bangla language boasts a rich literary heritage, shared with neighboring Bangladesh. West Bengal has a long tradition in folk literature, evidenced by the *Charyapada*, *Mangalkavya*, *Shreekrishna Kirtana*, *Thakurmar Jhuli*, and stories related to Gopal Bhar. In the nineteenth and twentieth century, Bengali literature was modernized in the works of authors such as Bankim Chandra Chattopadhyay, Michael Madhusudan Dutt, Rabindranath Tagore, Kazi Nazrul Islam and Sharat Chandra Chattopadhyay.

The Baul tradition is a unique heritage of Bangla folk music, which has also been influenced by regional music traditions. Other folk music forms include Gombhira and Bhawaiya. Folk music in West Bengal is often accompanied by the ektara, a one-stringed instrument. West Bengal also has an heritage in North Indian classical music. From the early 1990s, there has been an emergence and popularisation of new genres of music, including fusions of Baul and Jazz by several Bangla bands, as well as the emergence of what has been called *Jeebonmukhi Gaan* (a modern genre based on realism) by artists like Kabir Suman and bands like Chandrabindu.

Bengali dance forms draw from folk traditions, especially those of the tribal groups, as well as the broader Indian dance traditions. Chau dance of Purulia is a rare form of mask dance. Mainstream Hindi films are popular, as are films from the Bengali cinema industry, dubbed "Tollywood". Tollygunj in Kolkata is the location of Bengali movie studios and the name "Tollywood" (similar as Hollywood, USA) is derived from that name. The Bengali film industry is also known for art films. Its long tradition of filmmaking has produced acclaimed directors like Satyajit Ray, Mrinal Sen and Ritwik Ghatak. Contemporary directors include Buddhadev Dasgupta, Goutam Ghose, Aparna Sen and Rituparno Ghosh.

Rice and fish are traditional favourite foods, leading to a saying that in Bengali, *machhe bhate bangali*, that translates as "fish and rice make a Bengali". Meat production has increased significantly in recent years. Bengalis make distinctive sweetmeats from milk products, including *Roshogolla*, *Chomchom*, *Kalojam* and several kinds of *Pitha*. Bengal's vast repertoire of fish-based dishes includes hilsa preparations, a favourite among Bengalis. Popular street food includes Beguni, Kati roll, and phuchka. *Panta bhat* (rice soaked overnight in water) is a traditional dish consumed in rural areas.

Bengali women commonly wear the *sha°i* and the salwar kameez, often distinctly designed according to local cultural customs. In urban areas, many women and men wear Western attire. Among men, European dressing has greater acceptance. Men also wear traditional costumes such as the *Panjabi* with *dhuti* or *pyjama*, often on religious occasions. Durga Puja in October is the most popular festival in the West Bengal. Pohela Baishakh (the Bengali New Year), Rathayatra, Dolyatra or Basanta-Utsab, Nobanno, *Poush parbon* (festival of Poush), kalipuja, saraswatipuja, laxmipuja, Christmas, Eid-ul-Fitr and Eid-ul-Adha are other major festivals. Buddha Purnima, which marks the birth of Gautama Buddha, is one of the most important Buddhist festivals while Christmas, called *Boodin* (Great day) in Bangla is celebrated by the minority Christian population. West Bengal has been home to several famous religious teachers, including Sri Ramakrishna, and Swami Vivekananda and Sri Chaitanya.

MUSIC AND DANCE

Baul singers at Basanta-Utsab, Shantiniketan

Dance with Rabindra Sangeet

A notable music tradition is the Baul music, practiced by the Bauls, a sect of mystic minstrels.Other folk music forms include Gombhira and Bhawaiya. Folk music in West Bengal is often accompanied by the ektara, a one-stringed instrument. Shyama Sangeet is a genre of devotional songs, praising the Hindu goddess Kali; kirtan is devotional group songs dedicated to the god Krishna. Like other states in northern India, West Bengal also has a heritage in North Indian classical music. "Rabindrasangeet", songs composed and set into tune by Rabindranath Tagore, and "Nazrul geeti" (by Kazi Nazrul Islam) are popular. Also prominent are Dwijendralal, Atulprasad and Rajanikanta's songs, and *"adhunik"* or modern music from films and other composers. From the early 1990s, there has been an emergence of new genres of music, including what has been called Bengali *Jeebonmukhi Gaan* (a modern genre based on realism). Bengali dance forms draw from folk traditions, especially those of the tribal groups, as well as the broader Indian dance traditions. Chhau dance of Purulia is a rare form of masked dance.

Satyajit Ray, a pioneer in Bengali cinema along with Ravi Sankar

Films

Cinema of West Bengal is mostly shot in studios in the Kolkata neighbourhood of Tollygunj, and the name "Tollywood" (similar to Hollywood and Bollywood) is derived from that name. The Bengali film industry is well known for its art films, and has produced acclaimed directors like Satyajit Ray who is widely regarded as one of the greatest filmmakers of the 20th century, Mrinal Sen whose films were known for its artistic depiction of social reality, Tapan Sinha who was one of the most prominent Indian film directors of his time, and Ritwik Ghatak. Some contemporary directors include veterans such as Buddhadev Dasgupta, Tarun Majumdar, Goutam Ghose, Aparna Sen, and Rituparno Ghosh, and a newer pool of directors such as Kaushik Ganguly and Srijit Mukherji.

Reformist heritage

The capital, Kolkata, was the workplace of several social reformers, including Raja Ram Mohan Roy, Iswar Chandra Vidyasagar, and Swami Vivekananda. Their social reforms eventually led to a cultural atmosphere that made it possible for practices like sati, dowry, and caste-based discrimination, or untouchability, to be abolished. The region was also home to several religious teachers, such as Chaitanya, Ramakrishna, Prabhupada, and Paramahansa Yogananda.

Cuisine

Assorted food eaten in West Bengal: **Patisapta,** *a kind of pitha; Shorshe Ilish (Hilsha with Mustard Sauce) and Rasgullas in sugar syrup*

Rice and fish are traditional favourite foods, leading to a saying in Bengali, *machhe bhate bangali*, that translates as "fish and rice make a Bengali". Bengal's vast repertoire of fish-based dishes includes hilsa preparations, a favourite among

Bengalis. There are numerous ways of cooking fish depending on the fish's texture, size, fat content, and bones. Most of the people also consume eggs, chicken, mutton, and shrimp. *Panta bhat* (rice soaked overnight in water) with onion and green chili is a traditional dish consumed in rural areas, Common spices found in a Bengali kitchen are cumin, ajmoda (radhuni), bay leaf, mustard, ginger, green chillies, and turmeric. Sweets occupy an important place in the diet of Bengalis and at their social ceremonies. Bengalis make distinctive sweetmeats from milk products, including *Rôshogolla*, *Chômchôm*, *Kalojam*, and several kinds of *sondesh*. Pitha, a kind of sweet cake, bread, or dimsum, are specialties of the winter season. Sweets such as *narkol-naru*, *til-naru*, *moa*, and *payesh* are prepared during the festivals such as Lakshmi puja. Popular street foods include *Aloor Chop*, Beguni, Kati roll, biryani, and phuchka.

Clothing

Jamdani Sari of Bangladesh is very popular in West Bengal.

Bengali women commonly wear the *sari*, often distinctly designed according to local cultural customs. In urban areas, many women and men wear western attire. Among men, western dress has greater acceptance. Particularly on cultural occasions, men also wear traditional costumes such as the *panjabi* with *dhuti* while women wear *salwar kameez* or *sari*.

West Bengal produces several varieties of cotton and silk saris in the country. Handlooms are a popular way of livelihood to the rural population of the state. Every district has weaving "clusters", which are home to artisan communities, each specialising in specific varieties of handloom weaving. Notable handloom saris include *tant*, *jamdani*, *garad*, *korial*, *baluchari*, *tussar*, and muslin.

BENGALI CINEMA

The history of cinema in Bengal dates back to the 1890s, when the first "bioscopes" were shown in theatres in Kolkata. Within a decade, the first seeds of the industry was sown by Hiralal Sen, considered a stalwart of Victorian era cinema when he set up the Royal Bioscope Company, producing scenes from the stage productions of a number of popular shows at the Star Theatre, Minerva Theatre, Classic Theatre. Following a long gap after Sen's works, Dhirendra Nath Ganguly (Known as D.G) established Indo British Film Co., the first Bengali owned production company, in 1918.

However, the first Bengali Feature film, Billwamangal, was produced in 1919, under the banner of Madan Theatre. Bilat Ferat was the IBFC's first production in 1921. The New Theatre production of Dena Paona was the first Bengali talkie. A long history has been traversed since then, with stalwarts such as Satyajit Ray, Mrinal Sen and Ritwik Ghatak and others having earned international acclaim and securing their place in the movie history.

Today, there are two Bengali film industries, one in Dhaka, Bangladesh (called *Dhallywood*), and one in Kolkata, India. The film industry based in Kolkata is sometimes referred to as *Tollywood*, a portmanteau of the words *Tollygunge*, the area of South Kolkata where this industry is based, and *Hollywood*.

Motion Picture

Early History: Hiralal Sen is credited as one of Bengal's, and India's first directors. However, these were all silent films. Hiralal Sen is also credited as one of the pioneers of advertisement films in India. The first Bengali-language movie was the silent feature *Billwamangal*, produced by the Madan Theatre Company of Kolkata and released on November 8, 1919, only six years after the first full-length Indian feature film, *Raja Harish Chandra*, was released.

The early beginnings of the "talking film" industry go back to the early 1930's, when it came to British India, and to Kolkata. The movies were originally made in Urdu or Persian as to accommodate a specific elite market. One of the earliest known studios was the East India Film Company. The first Bengali film to be made as a talkie was an adaptation of Tagore's short story, Dena Paona, released in 1931.

It was at this time that the early heroes of the Bengali film industry like Pramathesh Barua and Debaki Bose were at the peak of their popularity. Barua also directed a number of movies, exploring new dimension in Indian cinema. Debaki Bose directed Chandidas in 1932; this film is noted for its breakthrough in recording sound. Sound recordist Mukul Bose found out solution to the problem of spacing out dialogue and frequency modulation.

The contribution of Bengali film industry to Indian film is quite significant. Based in Tollygunge, an area of South Kolkata, West Bengal and is more elite and artistically-inclined than the usual musical cinema fare in India. In the past, it enjoyed a large, even disproportionate, representation in Indian cinema, and produced film directors like Satyajit Ray, who was an Academy Honorary Award winner, and the recipient of India and France's greatest civilian honours, the Bharat Ratna and Legion of Honour respectively, and Mrinal Sen, who is the recipient of the French distinction of Commander of the Order of Arts and Letters and the Russian Order of Friendship.

Other prominent film makers in the Bengali film industry are Bimal Roy, the late Ritwik Ghatak, and Aparna Sen. The Bengali film industry has produced classics like 'Pather Panchali', 'Devi', 'Jalsaghar', 'Devdas', 'Neel Akasher Neechey', 'Meghe Dhaka Tara', etc.

The most well known Bengali filmstar to date has been Uttam Kumar; he and co-star Suchitra Sen were known as *The Eternal Pair*. The pioneers in Bengali film music include Raichand

Boral, Pankaj Mullick and K. C. Dey, all associated with New Theatres Kolkata. Other famous playback singers in Bengali film music were Hemanta Mukherjee, Manna Dey, Sandhya Mukhopadhyay and Kishore Kumar.

In the 1980s, however, the Bengal film industry went through a period of turmoil, with a shift from its traditional artistic and emotional inclinations to an approach more imitating the increasingly more popular Hindi films, along with a decline in the audience and critical appreciation, with notable exceptions of the works of directors like Gautam Ghose. However, even at this time, a number of actors and actresses enjoyed popularity, including Proshenjit, Chironjeet, Rituparna Sengupta and others.

However, toward the end of the 90s, with the a number of directors coming increasingly into prominence, including Rituparno Ghosh, Gautam Ghose, Aparna Sen, Sandip Ray among others, a number of popular and critically acclaimed movies have come out of the Bengali film industry in recent years. These include, Unishe April, Titli, Mr. and Mrs. Iyer, etc. and signal a resurgence of the Bengali film industry.

MUSIC

The music of Bengal, also referred to as Bangla music, comprises a long tradition of religious and secular song-writing over a period of almost a millennium. Composed with lyrics in the Bengali language, Bengali music spans a wide variety of styles, though it is most strongly affected by Hindustani music.

Styles: Bengal is today split between the Indian state of West Bengal and the independent nation of Bangladesh.

The earliest music in Bengal was influenced by Sanskrit chants, and evolved under the influence of Vishnu poetry such as the 13th-century *Gitagovindam* by Jayadeva, whose work continues to be sung in many eastern Hindu temples. The Middle Ages saw a mixture of Hindu and Islamic trends when the musical tradition was formalized under the patronage of Nawabs and the powerful landlords *bAro bhuiyAn*. Much of the early canon is devotional, as in the Hindu devotional songs of Ramprasad Sen, a bhakta who captures the Bengali ethos in his poetic, rustic,and ecstatic vision of the Hindu goddess of time and destruction in her motherly incarnation, Ma Kali. Another writer of the time was Vidyapati. Notable in this devotional poetry is an earthiness that does not distinguish between love in its carnal and devotional forms; some see connections between this and Tantra, which originated some time in the middle of the first millennium CE.

The Bauls (the word comes from Sanskrit *batul*, meaning "divinely inspired insanity") are a group of Hindu mystic minstrels from the Bengal region, who sang primarily in the 18th and 19th centuries.

They are thought to have been influenced greatly by the Hindu tantric sect of the Kartabhajas as well as by Sufi philosophers. Bauls traveled and sang in search of the internal ideal, *Moner Manush* (*Man of the Heart* or the *inner being*), and descried "superfluous" differences between religions. Lalon Fakir, alternatively known as Lalon Shah, who lived in the 19th century in and around Kushtia, is considered to be the greatest of all bauls.

By far the most defining expression of Bengali music, with an ouvre of over two thousand songs, was Rabindranath Tagore (known in Bengali as *Robi Thakur* and *Gurudeb*, the latter meaning "Divine Teacher"). His songs are affectionately called *Rabindrasangeet*, and cover topics from romantic love in a lush Bengali setting to universal love, often inspired by the lilas of Krishna and the transcendentalism of the Upanishads. Among the most notable Rabindrasangeet artists in West Bengal are Kanika Bandyopadhyay, Debobroto Biswas, Suchitra Mitra, and, more recently, Promita Mallik.

Another influential body of work is that of Kazi Nazrul Islam, which constitutes what is known as Nazrul geeti. The most notable Nazrul geeti singers are Firoza Begum, Anup Ghoshal, Sohrab Hossain.

Other Bengali music, shared by West Bengal and Bangladesh,

is from the poetry and songs of Nidhu Babu, Kabir, Lalon Fakir, Atulprasad Sen, Dvijendralal Roy, and a large canon of patriotic songs from Greater India's Independence movement.

Beginning with the establishment of Hindu Mela in 1867, the concept of patriotism entered Bengali music. The patriotic genre was a major part of Bengali music until its independence in 1947.

Modern Bengali music has been enriched by the likes of noted composer Salil Chowdhury, and singers Hemanta Mukhopadhaya, Sandhya Mukhopadhya, Manna Dey, Sabina Yasmin, and Runa Laila.

In recent times, western influence has resulted in the emergence of the phenomenon of Bangla bands, both in Dhaka and in Kolkata, as well as songs reflecting the joys and sorrows of the common man, *Jibonmukhi Gaan* (songs from life). Some famous Bangla bands are Bhoomi, Chandrabindoo, Miles, Nagar Baul, Feedback, Souls, Fossils, Cactus, Lakkihichara, Krosswindz and Insomnia. At the same time, singers like Ajoy Chakraborty are working to bring back classical raga influence into bengali music.

Rabindrasangeet

Rabindrasangeet refers to complete body of songs (approximmately 2230) and lyrical poetry written and composed by Bengali Nobel-laureate poet Rabindranath Tagore. The term refers to both the genre and the individual songs themselves.

These songs are regarded as cultural treasures of Bengal in both Bangladesh and West Bengal (India). The Rabindrasangeet, which deal with varied themes are immensely popular and form a foundation for the Bengali ethos that is comparable to, perhaps even greater than, that which Shakespeare has on the English-speaking world. It is said that his songs are the outcome of 500 years of literary & cultural churning that the Bengali community has gone through.

In his book *Caste and Outcaste*, Dhan Gopal Mukherjee has said that these songs transcend the mundane to the aesthetic and express all ranges and categories of human emotion. The poet had given a voice to all—big or small, rich or poor. The poorest boatman on the Ganges as well as the rich landlord find expression to their emotional trials and tribulation in the songs of Tagore. Rabindrasangeet has evolved into a distinctive school of music. Practitioners of this genre are known to be fiercely protective of tradionalist practice.

Novel interpretations and variations have drawn severe censure in both West Bengal and Bangladesh. And like Beethoven's symphonies or Vilayat Khan's sitar, Rabindrasangeet demands an educated, intelligent & cultured audience to appreciate the lyrical beauty of his compositions.

He was among the first to recognize that cinema should have its own language. In 1929 he wrote, "The beauty and grandeur of this form in motion has to be developed in such a way that it becomes self-sufficient without the use of words." The inherent beauty & depth of Tagore's songs have persuaded a number of filmmakers to use Tagore's songs in their films including Satyajit Ray, Ritwik Ghatak, Mrinal Sen, Nitin Bose, Tapan Sinha and Kumar Shahani. His songs were also used in British, European & Australian movies just to capture the mood of a cinematic situation & to reveal a delicate interplay of relationships.

Ritwik Ghatak said of Tagore, "That man has culled all my feelings from long before my birth...I read him and find that...I have nothing new to say." In his Meghe Dhaka Tara (The Cloud-capped Star) and Subarnarekha, Ghatak uses Rabindrasangeet to express the poignancy of post-Partition Bengal.

Two of the songs written by Tagore are the national anthems of India and Bangladesh. These are:

- *Bangladesh:* Amar Shonar Bangla
- *India:* Jana Gana Mana

Here is a good collection of free to download Rabindrasangeet. Most of them are quite good as far as technical quality is concerned.

Some of the well-known singers of Rabindrasangeet are:

- Pankaj Mullick also known as the *First Man* of Rabindrasangeet.
- Hemanta Kumar Mukhopadhyay
- Debabrata Biswas also known as the *Second Man* of Rabindrasangeet & unarguably the most popular among male voices.
- Subinoy Roy.
- Kanika Bandyopadhyay her original name was "Anima" but Tagore had renamed her "Kanika" and Abanindranath Tagore used to call her *Mohar* by which name she is known to many of her dedicated listeners.
- Suchitra Mitra
- Rajeshwari Dutta was originally from Punjab. She was married to a well-known Bengali poet, Sudhindranath Dutta. She made her mark in the classical-based *tappa* and other compositions
- Argha Sen
- Ashoketaru Bandyopadhyay
- Beethin Bandopadhyay
- Banani Ghosh
- Debabrata Biswas
- Dwijen Mukhopadhay
- Chinmay Chattopadhyay
- Gita Ghatak
- Iffatara Khan
- Mita Huq
- Neelima Sen
- Promita Mollik
- Purba Dam
- Rajasree
- Rajeswari Dutta
- Rezwana Chowdhury Banya
- Ritu Guha

- Roma Mondal
- Rono Gohathakurota
- Sadi Mohammad
- Sagar Sen
- Sumitra Sen
- Sanghamitramitra Gupta
- Susil Mullick
- Swagatalakshmi Dasgupta
- swapan Gupta

Some of the well-known teachers of Rabindrasangeet (barring Tagore himself) are:

- Dinendra Nath Tagore
- Shantideb Ghosh
- Ashoketaru Bandyopadhyay
- Dwijen Mukhopadhay
- Shailaja Ranjan Majumdar
- Maya Sen
- Suchitra Mitra
- Rajasree
- Kanika Bandyopadhyay
- Rezwana Chowdhury Banya
- Subinoy Roy
- Swagatalakshmi Dasgupta

Nazrul Geeti

Nazrul Geeti, (more appropriately, Nazrul Sangeet), literally meaning "music of Nazrul," are the works of Kazi Nazrul Islam, national poet of Bangladesh and active revolutionary during Indian Independence Movement. Nazrul Sangeet incorporate revolutionary notions as well as more spiritual, philosophical and romantic themes. Kazi Nazrul Islam used his music as a major way of disseminating his revolutionary notions, mainly by the use of strong words and powerful, but catchy, tunes. Among the revolutionary songs, *Karar Oi Louho Kopat* (Prison-doors of Steel) is best known and has been used in several movies, especially those made during the pre-independence period of Bangladesh.

Bangla Band

A Bangla band is any (modern) musical band that performs solely or mainly in the Bengali language and which uses Western principles of music.

Mohiner Ghoraguli is widely credited with being the first Bangla Band, though it did not achieve wide recognition in its time. Later, as Western influences became more widespread, the Bangla band became popular with young people during the 1980s and 1990s, both in India and Bangladesh, and has since become entrenched in modern Bengali culture.

Bangla bands use a wide variety of styles such as rock, pop, hard rock, heavy metal, grunge, folk, and fusion. Their music is influenced both by popular American music as well as traditional Bengali folk music such as shyama sangeet and baul. Like popular music in other countries, Bangla bands are very popular among Bengali young people.

BENGALI DANCE

Rabindra Nritya Natya: Rabindra nritya natya is the term given to the three dance-dramas composed by Bengal's poet laureate Rabindranath Tagore: *Chitrangada, Chandalika* and *Shyama*. The principal characteristic of these works is that the story is told entirely through dance and song. The dances included in them were in the dance form created by Tagore (see Tagore dance). Tagore also included dance in earlier works such as *Tasher Desh* (The country of cards), though these are not regarded as *Rabindra nritya natya*.

3

Government and Politics

INTRODUCTION

West Bengal is governed through a parliamentary system of representative democracy, a feature the state shares with other Indian states. Universal suffrage is granted to residents. There are two branches of government. The legislature, the West Bengal Legislative Assembly, consists of elected members and special office bearers such as the Speaker and Deputy Speaker, who are elected by the members. Assembly meetings are presided over by the Speaker or the Deputy Speaker in the Speaker's absence.

The judiciary is composed of the Calcutta High Court and a system of lower courts. Executive authority is vested in the Council of Ministers headed by the Chief Minister although the titular head of government is the Governor. The Governor is the head of state appointed by the President of India. The leader of the party or coalition with a majority in the Legislative Assembly is appointed as the Chief Minister by the Governor, and the Council of Ministers are appointed by the Governor on the advice of the Chief Minister. The Council of Ministers reports to the Legislative Assembly. The Assembly is unicameral with 295 Members of the Legislative Assembly, or MLAs, including one nominated from the Anglo-Indian community.

Terms of office run for five years, unless the Assembly is dissolved prior to the completion of the term. Auxiliary authorities known as *panchayats*, for which local body elections are regularly held, govern local affairs. The state contributes 42 seats to the Lok Sabha and 16 seats to the Rajya Sabha of the Indian Parliament.

Main offices in West Bengal

Raj Bhavan, the residence of the governor of the state

West Bengal Legislative Assembly

Calcutta High Court, highest court in West Bengal

Nabanna, Office of Chief Minister of West Bengal

Writers' Building, West Bengal Government Secretariat

The main players in the politics of the state are the All India Trinamool Congress, the Indian National Congress, and the Left Front alliance (led by the Communist Party of India (Marxist) or CPI(M)). Following the West Bengal State Assembly Election in 2011, the All India Trinamool Congress and Indian National Congress coalition under Mamata Banerjee of the All India Trinamool Congress was elected to power (getting 225 seats in the legislature). Prior to this, West Bengal was ruled by the Left Front for 34 years (1977–2011), making it the world's longest-running democratically elected communist government. Banerjee was re-elected as Chief Minister in the 2016 election in which Trinamool Congress won an absolute majority.

The state has one autonomous region, the Gorkhaland Territorial Administration.

GOVERNMENT OF WEST BENGAL

The Government of West Bengal also known as the State Government of West Bengal, or locally as State Government, is the supreme governing authority of the Indian state of West

Bengal and its 23 districts. It consists of an executive, led by the Governor of West Bengal, a judiciary and a legislative.

Like other states in India, the head of state of West Bengal is the Governor, appointed by the President of India on the advice of the Central government. His or her post is largely ceremonial. The Chief Minister is the head of government and is vested with most of the executive powers. Kolkata is the capital of West Bengal, and houses the Vidhan Sabha(Legislative Assembly). The secretariat is located in Howrah, in the Nabanna building. The Calcutta High Court is located in Kolkata, which has jurisdiction over the whole of West Bengal and the Andaman and Nicobar Islands.

The present Legislative Assembly of West Bengal is unicameral, consisting of 295 Member of the Legislative Assembly(M.L.A) including one nominated from the Anglo-Indian community. Its term is 5 years, unless sooner dissolved.

History

On 18 January 1862, under the Indian Councils Act of 1861, a 12-member Legislative Council for Bengal was founded by the Governor-General of India with the Lt Governor of Bengal and some nominated members.. The strength of this council was gradually increased by subsequent acts. Under the Indian Councils Act of 1892, the maximum strength of the council was increased to 20 members out of which seven members were to be elected. After the Indian Councils Act of 1909 the number raised to 50 members.

Council of Ministers

The West Bengal government headed by Mamata Banerjee has 41 ministers, including 17 new faces. Among them, 5 are Ministers of State holding independent charge, and 8 are junior ministers.

POLITICS OF WEST BENGAL

Politics in West Bengal is dominated by the following major political parties: the Communist Party of India (Marxist), the

Indian National Congress, the Bharatiya Janata Party and the Trinamool Congress.

In 1977 the Left Front won the state assembly elections, and the state was ruled by communists and other left groups till 2011. The erstwhile left front led West Bengal state government holds the Indian record for the longest period of governance.

Until 3 November 2000, Jyoti Basu was the Chief Minister of the state. After his resignation, due to health reasons, Buddhadeb Bhattacharjee became the Chief Minister of West Bengal who continued in office until 13 May 2011.

In the run-up to the 2011 elections, the state witnessed several violent clashes between the workers of the opposition parties and the ruling left party cadres.

In the 2011 Assembly Election, the Trinamool Congress-Indian National Congress alliance won by a huge margin with Mamata Banerjee becoming the first woman chief minister of West Bengal after 34 years of Communist rule.

In the 2016 Election, Congress and Left Front formed an alliance, and the election witnessed a three-way contest between their alliance, Trinamool Congress, and BJP.

DISTRICTS

As of 2017, West Bengal is divided into 23 districts.

Each district is governed by a district collector or district magistrate, appointed by either the Indian Administrative Service or the West Bengal Civil Service. Each district is subdivided into sub-divisions, governed by a sub-divisional magistrate, and again into blocks. Blocks consists of panchayats (village councils) and town municipalities.

The capital and largest city of the state is Kolkata – the third-largest urban agglomeration and the seventh-largest city in India. Asansol is the second-largest city and urban agglomeration in West Bengal after Kolkata. Siliguri is an economically important city, strategically located in the northeastern Siliguri Corridor (Chicken's Neck) of India. Other cities and towns in West Bengal with 2011 populations over 250,000 are Durgapur, Bardhaman, English Bazar, Baharampur, Habra, Kharagpur, and Shantipur.

A hut in a village in the Hooghly district

Subdivisions

There are 19 districts in West Bengal— Bankura, Bardhaman, Birbhum, Cooch Behar, Darjeeling, East Midnapore, Hooghly, Howrah, Jalpaiguri, Kolkata, Malda, Murshidabad, Nadia, North 24 Parganas, North Dinajpur, Purulia, South 24 Parganas, Dakshin Dinajpur and West Midnapore. Each district is governed by a district collector or district magistrate, appointed either by the Indian Administrative Service or the West Bengal Civil Service. Each district is subdivided into Sub-Divisions, governed by a sub-divisional magistrate, and again into Blocks. Blocks consists of panchayats (village councils) and town municipalities.

The capital and largest city of the state is Kolkata— the third-largest urban agglomeration and the fourth-largest city in India. Siliguri is an economically important town, strategically located in the northeastern Chicken's Neck of India. Asansol, Durgapur and Raniganj are cities in the western industrial belt. Other major cities and towns in West Bengal are Howrah, Haldia, Kharagpur, Burdwan, Darjeeling, Midnapore, Tamluk, Malda and Cooch Behar.

The Government of West Bengal also known as the State Government of West Bengal, or locally as State Government, is the supreme governing authority of the Indian state of West Bengal and its 19 districts.

It consists of an excecutive, led by the Governor of West Bengal, a judiciary and a legislative.

Like other states in India, the head of state of West Bengal is the Governor, appointed by the President of India on the advice of the Central government. His or her post is largely ceremonial. The Chief Minister is the head of government and is vested with most of the executive powers. Kolkata is the capital of West Bengal, and houses the Vidhan Sabha (Legislative Assembly) and the secratariat (Writers' Building).

The Kolkata High Court is located in Kolkata, which has jurisdiction over the whole of West Bengal and the Andaman and Nicobar Islands. The present Legislative Assembly of West Bengal is unicameral, consisting of 295 MLA including one nominated from the Anglo-Indian community. Its term is 5 years, unless sooner dissolved.

History: In 1912 the Imperial capital of India was moved from Kolkata to Delhi and as some compensation to Bengal the Lieutenant governor with Council gave place to a Governor with a Council thus completing the circle and reverting to the position which had been obtained 200 years ago. In 1947 India achieved independence and the title of governor of Bengal remained the same at it is to the present day.

Powers and Functions: The Governor enjoys many different types of powers:

- Executive powers related to administration, appointments and removals,

- Legislative powers related to lawmaking and the state legislature, that is Vidhan Sabha or Vidhan Parishad, and
- Discretionary powers to be carried out according to the discretion of the Governor.

Ex-officio Role of Governor

In his ex-officio capacity, the Governor of West Bengal is Chancellor of the universities of West Bengal (at present 14) as per the Acts of the Universities. The Universities are - University of Kolkata, Jadavpur University, University of Kalyani, Rabindra Bharati University, Vidyasagar University, University of Burdwan, North Bengal University, Netaji Subhas Open University, West Bengal University of Technology, Bengal Engineering & Science University, Uttar Banga Krishi Viswavidyalaya, Bidhan Chandra Krishi Viswavidyalaya, University of Animal and Fishery Sciences and West Bengal University of Health Sciences. For Visva Bharati, the Governor is the Pradhana (Rector).

The Governor is also the Chairman/President of some organizations such as Victoria Memorial Hall, Indian Museum, The Ramakrishna Mission Institute of Culture, Eastern Zonal Cultural Centre, Maulana Abul Kalam Azad Institute of Asian Studies (MAKAIAS), Kolkata Cultural Centre (Kolkata Kala Kendra), Special Fund for R&R of Ex-servicemen, West Bengal (Rajya Sainik Board), Sri Aurobindo Samiti, Indian Red Cross Society - West Bengal State Branch, St. John Ambulance Brigade No. II (West Bengal) District, Bharat Scouts and Guides and the Bengal Tuberculosis Association.

Governor of West Bengal's Welfare Fund, has the Governor as its Chairman. Contributions from this Fund are given to the needy people for meeting, to some extent the cost of their treatment. Besides the above, at his discretion, the Governor, accepts the position of Chief Patron/Patron or other posts in the honorary capacity, in various organizations that are rendering yeoman service to the society in different fields.

INDIAN POLITICAL PARTIES

West Bengal Socialist Party

West Bengal Socialist Party is a political party in the Indian state of West Bengal. WBSP was formed when the Bengali socialists split in the beginning of the 1980s (the other faction became the Democratic Socialist Party). WBSP is a part of Left Front. The party leader Kiranmoy Nanda is the Fisheries Minister in the West Bengal government. WBSP has sometimes threatened to leave Left Front.

In the state assembly elections 2001 WBSP launched four candidates, supported by Left Front. All four got elected. In total the party received 246 407 votes. In 2005 municipal polls in Kolkata WBSP contested 2 seats (ward no. 55 and 63) as a part of LF. It has lost both the seats.

In the 2006 West Bengal state assembly election, WBSP retained its four seats.

Workers Party of India

Workers Party of India, a political party in the Indian state of West Bengal. WPI has its origin in the Democratic Vanguard in India. DV was formed in 1943 when a group led by Jiban Lal Chattopadhyay broke away from the Radical Democratic Party of M.N. Roy. DV were dissatified with the development of RDP into a non-Marxist outfit. Jiban Lal Chattopadhyay had been elected secretary of the Bengal Congress in 1930.

In 1960 DV became the Workers Party of India. WPI was part of the CPI(M)-led United Front, which governed West Bengal 1967-1971. Jiban Lal Chattopadhyay died in 1970. In 1976 WPI split into two. The major faction, led by Monidranarayan Basu, retained the name WPI. The minor faction called itself Communist Workers Party.

Basu died in a car accident, and Salien Pal took over the leadership. WPI publishes *Ganabiplab* (Popular Revolution) in Bengali.

WPI has choosed to stay out of the Left Front. WPI considers CPSU as revisionist.

Left Front

Left Front is an alliance of Indian leftist parties. In West Bengal and Tripura there are state-level committees of the Left Front. Currently Left Front governments rule both states.

In West Bengal the following parties are part of the Left Front:

- Communist Party of India (Marxist)
- Communist Party of India
- Revolutionary Socialist Party
- All India Forward Bloc
- Revolutionary Communist Party of India
- Marxist Forward Bloc
- West Bengal Socialist Party
- Democratic Socialist Party
- UTUC
- Biplobi Bangla Congress

Communist Revolutionary League of India was a member of the Bengali LF between 1995 and 2000.

The convenor of the West Bengal Left Front committee is Biman Bose, politburo member of CPI(M).

In Tripura, CPI(M), CPI, RSP and AIFB are members of Left Front.

In Kerala, a formation of left parties led by the CPI(M) called the Left Democratic Front is the governing group in the Kerala State Assembly.

In Tamil Nadu, left parties form part of the Progressive Democratic Alliance along with the regionalist DMK.

In Maharashtra, parties such as the Peasants and Workers Party of India, Kamgar Aghadi and Shetkari Sangh are the allies of the Left Front.

Communist Party of India (Marxist)

The Communist Party of India (Marxist) (usually abbreviated to CPI(M) or CPM) is a political party in India. It is strongest in the states of Kerala, West Bengal and Tripura. In all of these states, as of 2006, it currently holds the government. It split from the Communist Party of India in 1964. CPI(M) claims to have 814,408 members as of 2002.

History: Split in the Communist Party of India and formation of CPI(M)

CPI(M) emerged out of a division within the Communist Party of India (CPI). The undivided CPI had experienced a period of upsurge during the years following the Second World War. The CPI led armed rebellions in Telangana, Tripura and Kerala. However, it soon abandoned the strategy of armed revolution in favour of working within the parliamentary framework. In 1950 B. T. Ranadive, the CPI general secretary and a prominent representative of the radical sector inside the party, was demoted on grounds of left-adventurism.

Under the government of the Congress Party of Jawaharlal Nehru, independent India embarked developed close relations and a strategic partnership with the Soviet Union. The Soviet government consequently wished that the Indian communists moderate their criticism towards the Indian state and assume a supportive role towards the Congress governments. However, large sections of the CPI claimed that India remained a semi-feudal country, and that class struggle could not be put on the back-burner for the sake of guarding interests of Soviet trade and foreign policy. Moreover the Indian National Congress appeared to be generally hostile towards political competition. In 1959 the central government intervened to impose President's Rule in Kerala, toppling the E.M.S. Namboodiripad cabinet (the sole non-Congress state government in the country).

Simultaneously, the relations between the Communist Party of the Soviet Union and the Communist Party of China soured. In the early 1960s the Communist Party of China began criticising the CPSU of turning revisionist and of deviating from the path of Marxism-Leninism. Sino-Indian relations also deteriorated, as border disputes between the two countries erupted into the Indo-China war of 1962. During the war, the pro-Soviet faction of the Indian communists backed the position of the Indian government, while other sections of the party claimed that it was a conflict between a socialist and a capitalist state, and thus took a pro-Chinese position. Hundreds of CPI leaders, such as E. M. S. Namboodiripad and B. T. Ranadive, accused of being pro-Chinese were imprisoned. Thousands of communists were detained without trial. Those targeted by the state accused the pro-Soviet leadership of the CPI of conspiring with the Congress government to ensure their own hegemony over the control of the party.

In 1962 Ajoy Ghosh, the general secretary of the CPI, passed away. After his death, S. A. Dange was installed as the party chairman (a new position) and E. M. S. Namboodiripad as general secretary. This was an attempt to achieve a compromise. Dange represented the rightist fraction of the party and E. M. S. the leftist fraction.

At a CPI National Council meeting held on April 11, 1964, 32 Council members walked out in protest, accusing Dange and his followers of "anti-unity and anti-Communist policies".

The leftist section, to which the 32 National Council members belong, organised a convention in Tenali, Andhra Pradesh July 7 to 11. In this convention the issues of the internal disputes in the party were discussed. 146 delegates, claiming to represent 100,000 CPI members, took part in the proceedings. The convention decided to convene the 7th Party Congress of CPI in Kolkata later the same year.

Marking a difference from the Dangeite sector of CPI, the Tenali convention was marked by the display of a large portrait of the Chinese communist leader Mao Zedong.

At the Tenali convention a Bengal-based pro-Chinese group, representing one of the most radical streams of the CPI leftwing, presented a draft programme proposal of their own. These radicals criticised the draft programme proposal prepared by

M. Basavapunniah for undermining class struggle and failing to take a clear pro-Chinese position in the ideological conflict between CPSU and CPC.

After the Tenali convention the CPI leftwing organised party district and state conferences. In West Bengal, a few of these meetings became battlegrounds between the most radical elements and the more moderate leadership. At the Kolkata Party District Conference an alternative draft programme was presented to the leadership by Parimal Das Gupta (a leading figure amongst far-left intellectuals in the party). Another alternative proposal was brought forward to the Kolkata Party District Conference by Azizul Haque, but Haque was initially banned from presenting it by the conference organisers. At the Kolkata Party District Conference 42 delegates opposed M. Basavapunniah's official draft programme proposal.

At the Siliguri Party District Conference, the main draft proposal for a party programme was accepted, but with some additional points suggested by the far-left North Bengal cadre Charu Majumdar. However, Harekrishna Konar (representing the leadership of the CPI leftwing) forbade the raising of the slogan *Mao Tse-Tung Zindabad* (Long live Mao Tse-Tung) at the conference.

Parimal Das Gupta's document was also presented to the leadership at the West Bengal State Conference of the CPI leftwing. Das Gupta and a few other spoke at the conference, demanding the party ought to adopt the class analysis of the Indian state of the 1951 CPI conference. His proposal was, however, voted down.

The Kolkata Congress was held between October 31 and November 7, at Tyagraja Hall in southern Kolkata. Simultaneously, the Dange group convened a Party Congress of CPI in Bombay. Thus, the CPI divided into two separate parties. The group which assembled in Kolkata decided to adopt the name 'Communist Party of India (Marxist)', in order to differentiate themselves from the Dange group. The CPI(M) also adopted its own political programme. P. Sundarayya was elected general secretary of the party.

In total 422 delegates took part in the Kolkata Congress. CPI(M) claimed that they represented 104,421 CPI members, 60% of the total party membership.

At the Kolkata conference the party adopted a class analysis of the character of the Indian state, that claimed the Indian big bourgeoisie was increasingly collaborating with imperialism.

Parimal Das Gupta's alternative draft programme was not circulated at the Kolkata conference. However Souren Basu, a delegate from the far-left stronghold Darjeeling, spoke at the conference asking why no portrait had been raised of Mao Tse-Tung along the portraits of other communist stalwarts. His intervention has met with huge applauses from the delegates of the conference.

Early Years of CPI(M): The CPI(M) was born into a hostile political climate. At the time of the holding of its Kolkata Congress, large sections of its leaders and cadres were jailed without trial. Again on December 29-30, over a thousand CPI(M) cadres were arrested, and held in jail without trial. In 1965 new waves of arrests of CPI(M) cadres took place in West Bengal, as the party launched agitations against the rise in fares in the Kolkata Tramways and against the then prevailing food crisis. State-wide general strikes and hartals were observed on August 5, 1965, March 10-11, 1966 and April 6, 1966. The March 1966 general strike results in several deaths in confrontations with police forces.

Also in Kerala, mass arrests of CPI(M) cadres were carried out during 1965. In Bihar, the party called for a *Bandh* (general strike) in Patna on August 9, 1965 in protest against the Congress state government. During the strike, police resorted to violent actions against the organisers of the strike. The strike was followed by agitations in other parts of the state.

The Central Committee of CPI(M) held its first meeting on June 12-19 1966. The reason for delaying the holding of a regular CC meeting was the fact that several of the persons elected as CC members at the Calcutta Congress were jailed at the time. A CC meeting had been scheduled to have been held in Trichur during the last days of 1964, but had been cancelled due to the wave of arrests against the party.

1967 General Election: In the 1967 Lok Sabha elections CPI(M) nominated 59 candidates. In total 19 of them were elected. The party received 6.2 million votes (4.28% of the nationwide vote). By comparison, CPI won 23 seats and got 5.11% of the nation-wide vote. In the state legistative elections held simultaneously, the CPI(M) emerged as a major party in Kerala and West Bengal. In Kerala a United Front government led by E. M. S. Namboodiripad was formed. In West Bengal, CPI(M) was the main force behind the United Front government formed. The Chief Ministership was given to Ajoy Mukherjee of the Bangla Congress (a regional splinter-group of the Indian National Congress).

Naxalbari Uprising: At this point the party now stood at a crossroad. Some sectors were wary of the increasing parliamentary focus of the party leadership, especially after the electoral victories in West Bengal and Kerala. Developments in China also affected the situation inside the party. In West Bengal two separate internal dissident tendencies emerged, which both could be identified as supporting the Chinese line. In 1967 a peasant uprising broke out in Naxalbari, in northern West Bengal.

The insurgency was led by hardline district-level CPI(M) leaders Charu Majumdar and Kanu Sanyal. The hardliners within CPI(M) saw the Naxalbari uprising as the spark that would ignite the Indian revolution. The Communist Party of China hailed the Naxalbari movement, causing an abrupt break in CPI(M)-CPC relations. The Naxalbari movement was violently repressed by the West Bengal government, of which CPI(M) was a major partner. Within the party, the hardliners rallied around an All India Coordination Committee of Communist Revolutionaries.

Following the 1968 Burdwan plenum of CPI(M) (held on April 5-12, 1968), the AICCCR separated themselves from CPI(M). This splits divided the party throughout the country.

But notably in West Bengal, which was the epicentre of the violent radicalist stream, no prominent leading figure left the party.

The party and the Naxalites (as the rebels were called) were soon to get into a bloody feud, a conflict which continues until today.

In Andhra Pradesh another revolt was taking place. There the pro-Naxalbari dissidents had not established any presence.

But in the party organisation there were many veterans from the Telangana armed struggle, who rallied against the central party leadership. In Andhra Pradesh the radicals had a strong base even amongst the state-level leadership.

The main leader of the radical tendency was T. Nagi Reddy, a member of the state legislative assembly. On June 15, 1968 the leaders of the radical tendency published a press statement outlining the critique of the development of CPI(M).

It was signed by T. Nagi Reddy, D. V. Rao, Kolla Venkaiah and Chandra Pulla Reddy. In total around 50% of the party cadres in Andhra Pradesh left the party to form the Andhra Pradesh Coordination Committee of Communist Revolutionaries, under the leadership of T. Nagi Reddy.

Dismissal of United Front Governments in West Bengal: In November 1967, the West Bengal United Front government was dismissed by the central government. Initially the Indian National Congress formed a minority government led by P. C. Joshi, but that cabinet did not last long. Following the proclamation that the United Front government had been dislodged, a 48-hartal was effective throughout the state. After the fall of the Joshi cabinet, the state was but under President's Rule. CPI(M) launched agitations against the interventions of the central government in West Bengal.

Elections in West Bengal and Kerala: Fresh elections were held in West Bengal in 1969. CPI(M) contested 97 seats, and won 80. The party was now the largest in the West Bengal legislative. But with the active support of CPI and the Bangla

Congress, Ajoy Mukherjee was returned as Chief Minister of the state.

Mukherjee resigned on March 16 1970, after a pact had been reached between CPI, Bangla Congress and the Indian National Congress against CPI(M). CPI(M) strove to form a new government, instead but the central government put the state under President's Rule.

Formation of CITU: Following the 1964 split, CPI(M) cadres had remained active with the All India Trade Union Congress. But as relations between CPI and CPI(M) soured, with the backdrop of confrontations in West Bengal and Kerala, a split also surfaced in the AITUC.

In December 1969, eight CPI(M) members walked out of a AITUC Working Committee meeting. The eight called for an All India Trade Union Convention, which was held in Goa April 9-10, 1970. The convention decided that, All India Trade Union Conference be held on May 28-31 in Calcutta. The Calcutta conference would be the founding conference of the Centre of Indian Trade Unions, a new pro-CPI(M) trade union movement.

Outbreak of War in East Pakistan: In 1971 Bangladesh (formerly East Pakistan) declared its independence from Pakistan. The Pakistani military tried to quell the uprising.

India intervened militarily and gave active backing to the Bangladeshi resistance. Millions of Bangladeshi refugees sought shelter in India, especially in West Bengal. CPI(M) embarked upon a massive relief effort, mobilizing its cadres to work in the refugee camps.

At the time the radical sections of the Bangladeshi communist movement was divided into many factions.

Whilst the pro-Soviet Communist Party of Bangladesh actively participated in the resistance struggle, the pro-China communist tendency found itself in a peculiar situation as China had sided with Pakistan in the war.

In Kolkata, were many Bangladeshi leftists had sought refugee, CPI(M) worked to coordinate the efforts to create a new political organization.

In the fall of 1971 three small groups, which were all hosted by the CPI(M), came together to form the Bangladesh Communist Party (Leninist). The new party became the sister party of CPI(M) in Bangladesh.

1971 General Election: With the backdrop of the Bangladesh War and the emerging role of Indira Gandhi as a populist national leader, the 1971 election to the Lok Sabha was held.

CPI(M) contested 85 seats, and won in 25. In total the party mustered 7510089 votes (5.12% of the national vote). 20 of the seats came from West Bengal (including Somnath Chatterjee, elected from Burdwan), 2 from Kerala (including A. K. Gopalan, elected from Trichur), 2 from Tripura (Biren Dutta and Dasarath Deb) and 1 from Andhra Pradesh.

In the same year, state legislative elections were held in three states; West Bengal, Tamil Nadu and Orissa. In West Bengal CPI(M) had 241 candidates, winning 113 seats. In total the party mustered 4241557 votes (32.86% of the state-wide vote).

In Tamil Nadu CPI(M) contested 37 seats, but drew blank. The party got 259298 votes (1.65% of the state-wide vote). In Orissa the party contested 11 seats, and won in two. The CPI(M) vote in the state was 52785 (1.2% of the state-wide vote).

1970s, 1980s, 1990s: In the 1977 election, the CPI(M) finally gained the majority in the Legislative Assembly of the State of West Bengal, defeating the Congress(I). Jyoti Basu became the chief minister of West Bengal, an office he held until his retirement. The CPI(M) has held the majority in the West Bengal government continuously since 1977.

Party Organization: CPI(M) got 5.66% of votes polled in last parliamentary election (May 2004) and it has 43 MPs. It won 42.31% on an average in the 69 seats it contested. It supports the new Indian National Congress-led United Progressive Alliance government, but without becoming a part of it.

In West Bengal and Tripura it participates in the Left Front. In Kerala the party is part of the Left Democratic Front. In Tamil Nadu it is part of the Progressive Democratic Alliance.

Leadership: The current general secretary of CPI(M) is Prakash Karat. The CPI(M) MP Somnath Chatterjee is the speaker of the Lok Sabha (2004). The 18th party congress of CPI(M), held in Delhi April 6-11 2005 elected a Central Committee with 85 members. The Central Committee later elected a 17-member Politburo:

- Harkishan Singh Surjeet
- Jyoti Basu
- V. S. Achuthanandan
- Prakash Karat
- Sitaram Yechury
- S. Ramachandran Pillai
- R. Umanath
- Anil Biswas (died on March 26, 2006)
- Biman Bose
- Manik Sarkar
- Pinarai Vijayan
- M. K. Pandhe
- Buddhadeb Bhattacharya
- Chittabrata Mazumdar (died on February 20, 2007)
- K. Varadarajan
- B. V. Raghavulu
- Brinda Karat

The principal mass organizations of CPI(M)

- Democratic Youth Federation of India
- Students Federation of India
- Centre of Indian Trade Unions class organisation
- All India Kisan Sabha peasants' organization
- All India Agricultural Workers Union
- All India Democratic Women's Association

- Bank Employees Federation of India
- All India Lawyers Union

In Tripura, the Ganamukti Parishad is a major mass organization amongst the tribal peoples of the state. In Kerala the Adivasi Kshema Samithi, a tribal organisation is controlled by CPI(M).

This apart, on the cultural front as many as 12 major organisations are led by CPI(M).

Party Publications: From the Centre, two weekly newspapers are published, *People's Democracy* (English) and *Lok Lehar* (Hindi). The central theoretical organ of the party is *Marxist*, published quarterly in English.

Daily Newspapers:

- Ganashakti (West Bengal, Bengali)
  Deshabhimani (Kerala), Malayalam)
- Daily Desher Katha (Tripura, Bengali)
- Theekathir (Tamil Nadu, Tamil)
- Prajashakti (Andhra Pradesh, Telugu)

Weeklies:

- Abshar (West Bengal, Urdu)
- Swadhintha (West Bengal, Hindi)
- Desh Hiteshi (Bengali)
- Aikya Ranga (Karnataka, Kannada)
- Jeevan Marg (Maharashtra, Marathi)
- Samyabadi (Orissa, Oriya)
- Deshabhimani Vaarika (Kerala), Malayalam)

Fortnightlies:

- Lok Jatan (Madhya Pradesh, Hindi)
- Lok Samvad (Uttar Pradesh, Hindi)
- Sarfarosh Chintan (Gujarat, Gujarati)

Monthlies:

- Shabtaab (Urdu)
- Yeh Naya Raste (Jammu & Kashmir, Urdu)

- Lok Lahar (Punjabi)
- Nandan (Bengali)
- Marxist (Tamil language)

Ideological Publications:

- Marxist (English)
- Marxvadi Path (Bengali)
- Chinta (Malayalam)
- Marxist (Telugu)

Publishing Houses:

- Leftword Books
- CPI(M) Publication
- National Book Agency (West Bengal)
- Chinta Publication (Kerala)
- Prajasakti Book House (Andhra Pradesh)
- Deshabhimani Book House (Kerala)

Name: During the initial period after the split 1964, the party was often referred to as 'Left Communist Party' or 'Communist Party of India (Left)'. The CPI was then, in the same parlance, dubbed as the 'Rightist Communist Party'.

Splits and Offshoots: A large number of parties have been formed as a result of splits from the CPI(M), such as Communist Party of India (Marxist-Leninist), Marxist Communist Party of India, Marxist Coordination Committee in Jharkhand, Janathipathiya Samrakshana Samithy, Communist Marxist Party and BTR-EMS-AKG Janakeeya Vedi in Kerala, Party of Democratic Socialism in West Bengal, Janganotantrik Morcha in Tripura, the Ram Pasla group in Punjab, Orissa Communist Party in Orissa, etc.

Akhil Bharatiya Gorkha League

Akhil Bharatiya Gorkha League is a political party working amongst the Nepali-speaking population in northern West Bengal, India. The party was founded in 1943 by Damber Singh Gurung. The current general secretary is Amar Lama.

ABGL is a part of the People's Democratic Front, an alliance led by the Communist Party of Revolutionary Marxists. PDF constists of parties who work for Gorkha autonomy but are opposed to the Gorkha National Liberation Front.

ABGL has two out of 28 seats in the Darjeeling Gorkha Hill Council. Perhaps a party branch will be founded in Sikkim. ABGL had a branch there in the 1970s.

Bangla Bachao Front

Bangla Bachao Front (Save Bengal Front), a front of opposition parties contesting the 2001 West Bengal legislative assembly elections. The front was led by All India Trinamool Congress and also included Bharatiya Janata Party, the Jharkhand Party, the Kamtapur Peoples Party, Samata Party and a break-away group of Biplobi Bangla Congress.

The front gave support to Gorkha National Liberation Front candidates in three constituencies.

Bangla Congress

Bangla Congress, regional political party in the Indian state of West Bengal. Bangla Congress was formed through a split in the Indian National Congress in the 1960s. 1967-1969, 1969-1971 BC was a part of the United Front governments in the state, co-governing with the Left. Ajoy Mukherjee, the BC leader, was the Chief Minister. In 1971 the alliance with the Left was broken, and without the support if CPI(M) the rule of Bangla Congress declined rapidly. BC was reunified with Congress. Ajoy Mukherjee died in 1986.

Electoral results from the West Bengal state assembly elections:

1967: 80 candidates, 34 elected, 1 286 028 votes

1969: 49 candidates, 33 elected, 1 094 654 votes

1971: 137 candidates, 5 elected, 695 376 votes

Lok Sabha election results:

1967: 7 candidates, 5 elected, 1 204 356 votes

1971: 14 candidates, 1 elected, 518 781 votes

Bharatiya Gorkha Janashakti

Bharatiya Gorkha Janashakti (Indian Gorkha People's Power), a political party in the northern parts of the Indian state of West Bengal. BGJS was launched in 1998, anticipating the 1999 Darjeeling Gorkha Autonomous Hills Council elections. BGJS was part of the United Front launched by Communist Party of Revolutionary Marxists and Akhil Bharatiya Gorkha League.

BGJS demanded that the Gorkhas should be included as Scheduled Tribes (giving access to quotas and reservations) and that the area of DHAGC ought to be reorganized.

In 2003 BGJS was revived, ahead of the DGAHC polls the following year.

Biplobi Bangla Congress

Biplobi Bangla Congress (Revolutionary Bengali Congress), political party in West Bengal, India. Emerged as a splinter-group of Bangla Congress ahead of the 1971 elections. BBC is led by Sunil Chaudhury and is part of the Left Front.

Around March 2001 there were reports that BBC would have switched sides and allied themselves with the All India Trinamool Congress and formed part of the Bangla Bachao Front.

But in the actual elections BBC was part of Left Front. Most probably it was a break-away group that had sided with Trinamool. Makhanlal Bangal, who in 1996 had been elected to the state assembly as a BBC candidate (and later got disqualified for electoral malpractice) was an AITC candidate in the 2001 state elections.

In the 2001 assembly elections of West Bengal, BBC contested the Sabong seat in Midnapore and its candidate Tushar Kanti Laya won it. In the 2005 Kolkata Municipal polls, BBC has contested 1 seat as part of Left Front. Its candidate Rita Chowdhury has been elected from ward no 41.

In the 2006 assembly elections of West Bengal, BBC again contested the Sabong seat with Tushar Kanti Laya as its candidate (on a CPI(M) symbol). Laya got 62079 votes (44.98%), but lost the seat to a Congress candidate.

Communist Party of Revolutionary Marxists

Communist Party of Revolutionary Marxists, is a political party in the northern areas of the Indian state of West Bengal. CPRM was formed in 1996 by Communist Party of India (Marxist)-dissidents (a major party of the local CPI(M) leadership in Darjeeling), who were dissatisfied with the peace treaty with the Gorkha National Liberation Front.

CPRM struggles for a separate Gorkhaland state to be formed within India. It contested the Darjeeling Gorkha Autonomous Hills Council in 1999, but won no seat. Before 1999 one CPRM member was sitting in DGAHC.

Ahead of the 1999 DGHC elections CPRM had participated in a United Front comprising of CPRM, Akhil Bharatiya Gorkha League, Indian National Congress, Bharatiya Gorkha Janashakti, Communist Party of India, All India Trinamool Congress, Bharatiya Nepali Bir Gorkha and Sikkim Rashtriya Mukti Morcha. In this front, only ABGL won any seats.

Since the failure of the United Front, CRPM has formed the People's Democratic Front, as a united opposition to GNLF in the Darjeeling Hills, together with Akhil Bharatiya Gorkha League, Indian National Congress, Gorkha National Liberation Front and Bharatiya Janata Party.

The youth organization of CPRM is called Democratic Revolutionary Youth Federation.

Communist Revolutionary League of India

Communist Revolutionary League of India a smaller political party in the Indian state of West Bengal. The party is led by Ashim Chatterjee, former student leader of Communist Party of India (Marxist-Leninist).

Chattejee broke with Charu Majumdar in 1971 after the failure of the attempts to build an armed movement in the Debra-Gopiballavbur area in West Bengal and due to the opposition of CPI(ML) towards the liberation struggle of Bangladesh.

Chatterjee formed the Bengal-Bihar-Orissa Border Regional Committee, CPI(ML). His group joined the CPI(ML) of Satayanarayan Singh. Later Chatterjee formed the CRLI.

During the period of 1995-2000 CRLI was member of Left Front. After breaking with CPI(M) CRLI has been in contact with the Party of Democratic Socialism of Saifuddin Chaudhury.

In the 2005 West Bengal Legislative Assembly elections, CRLI leader Chatterji contested on the election symbol of Trinamool Congress.

Communist Workers Party (India)

Communist Workers Party, a political party in the Indian state of West Bengal. CWP was formed by Jyotibhushan Bhattachayya, when the Workers Party of India split in 1976. Bhattachayya was a professor of English at Kolkata University and in 1967 he had become the first non-Congress Education Minister of West Bengal. CWP still exists, but its strength is minimal.

Democratic Socialist Party (Prabodh Chandra)

Democratic Socialist Party is a social democratic political party in India. The party is almost completely limited to West Bengal. The party was formed when the Bengali socialists, that had been part of Janata Party, were divided in two in the beginning of the 1980s. The other faction became the West Bengal Socialist Party.

DSP is part of the Left Front-government in West Bengal. The party leader Prabodh Chandra Sinha, is Minister of Parliamentary Affairs in the state government. Sinha was elected to the state assembly in 2001 as an independent candidate from the constituency Egra. At that time DSP was not registered at the Election Commission of India. Now the party has once again registered, under the name Democratic Socialist Party (Prabodh Chandra).

Prabodh Chandra Sinha was at a conference in New York during the September 11, 2001 attacks.

DSP has tried to contact the Socialist International, but have been denied membership on the grounds that they are a regional party. DSP has won the Pingla seat in 2006 assembly poll in West Bengal. Probodh Sinha lost his Egra seat to Trinamul's Sisir Adhikari.

Dr. Syamaprasad Jana Jagaran Manch

Dr. Syamaprasad Jana Jagaran Manch, a forum of BJP dissidents in the Indian state of West Bengal. The forum was launched on December 5, 2004 by former Union Minister Tapan Sikdar.

The organisation held its first convention in Kolkata on March 8, 2006. The forum is named after Syama Prasad Mukherjee, the founder of Bharatiya Jana Sangh. Sikdar maintains that the organisation is apolitical (in the sense that it is not a political party), and that he still sympathises with BJP. The group campaigns against Bangladeshi immigration to West Bengal.

Former senior BJP leader K. N. Govindacharya is associated with the group

Forward Bloc (Socialist)

Forward Bloc (Socialist), a break-away group from the All India Forward Bloc. FB(S) existed around 1996-1998. The party was primarily based in northern West Bengal.

In the Lok Sabha elections 1996 FB(S) had launched two candidates from West Bengal. Hiten Barman from Cooch Behar got 145 078 votes (15,56%) and Mihir Kumar Roy got 27 607 votes (3,09%) in Jalpaiguri. In the state Legislative Assembly election in West Bengal 1996, FB(S) had launched 20 candidates, who together got 123 316 votes. One candidate got elected, Kamal Guha from Dinhata (70 531 votes, 49,58%).

In the Lok Sabha elections 1998 FB(S) was with the Indian National Congress. The party launched one candidate in Cooch

Behar, north West Bengal, supported by Congress. The candidate, Gobinda Roy, came second with 272 974 votes (30,16%). Later FB(S) and AIFB were reunited.

Today Kamal Guha is the Agriculture minister of West Bengal and state president of AIFB.

Gorkha National Liberation Front

Gorkha National Liberation Front (GNLF) is a political party in northern West Bengal, India, formed in 1980. It is led by Subash Ghising.

During the 1980s the GNLF led an intensive and often violent campaign for the creation of a separate Gorkha state in the Nepali-speaking areas in northern West Bengal. The movement reached its peak around 1985-1986. The political violence in the area took thousands of lives during these years.

Ghising has also been accused of being a RAW agent in the Illustrated Weekly to keep the Southeast Asian-looking peoples in the hills at a check.

On the 22 August 1988 GNLF signed the *Darjeeling Hill Accord*. The treaty meant the creation of a *Darjeeling Gorkha Hill Council*, whilst GNLF would give up the demand for Gorkhaland.

In the year 2000 GNLF revived the demand for Gorkhaland in their political agitation.

In the state assembly elections in West Bengal in 2001 GNLF had put up five candidates, out of whom three got elected. In total the party received 190 057 votes.

GNLF boycotted the Lok Sabha elections 1996, 1998 and 1999. Ahead of the 2004 Lok Sabha elections GNLF supported Congress candidate Dawa Narbula, who won with large margin in the Darjeeling constituency.

GNLF runs the Darjeeling Gorkha Autonomous Hill Council and Ghising is the chairman of the council.

The 6th schedule has been signed between the central government, the state government and Subash Ghising as an individual (no longer an elected representative but in an appointed post) which according to the Constitution of India is illegal.

GNLF also has a branch in Sikkim.

Gorkha National Liberation Front (C. K. Pradhan)

Gorkha National Liberation Front (C. K. Pradhan), splinter-group of Gorkha National Liberation Front. GNLF(C) was formed in 2002 after the murder of GNLF leader C. K. Pradhan. Pradhan's widow, Sheila Pradhan, claims that he was killed by GNLF, since he was about to break away from the party.

After the assassination Sheila and other floated GNLF(C). The party is led by D. K. Pradhan, member of the West Bengal legislative assembly from Darjeeling.

GNLF(C) is a member of the People's Democratic Front, an alliance of parties in the Darjeeling area opposed to Ghising's GNLF.

Indian People's Forward Bloc

Indian People's Forward Bloc is a political party in West Bengal, India. The party emerged through a split in the All India Forward Bloc. The party is led by Jayanta Roy, former AIFB Rajya Sabha member, and Chhaya Ghosh, former West Bengal Minister of Agriculture. Ahead of the 2006 legislative election, IPFB reached an alliance with the Indian National Congress. No IPFB candidate got elected though.

Jana Unnayan Mancha

Jana Unnayan Mancha, a registered political party in the Indian state of West Bengal. JUM is the political front of Federation of Consumer Associations, West Bengal. The state secretary of JUM is Ramanimohan Nag Chowdhury, a retired senior officer of the Central Bureau of Investigation. JUM won three seats in the 2003 panchayat (local council) elections.

JUM launched one candidate in the 2006 West Bengal legislative election, Mala Banerjee in Diamond Harbour. Banerjee got 613 votes (0.48%).

Kamtapur People's Party

Kamtapur Peoples Party, is a political party working in the northern parts of the Indian state of West Bengal. KPP was founded in January 1996 by Atul Roy. KPP works amongst the Rajbanshi population. KPP demands the set-up of a separate Kamtapur state and recognition of the dialect of the Rajbanshis as a separate language.

KPP is alleged to be the political wing of the terrorist outfit Kamtapur Liberation Organization. The student wing of KPP is the All Kamtapur Students Union. The women's wing is called Kamtapur Women's Rights Forum.

Ahead of the 2001 West Bengal assembly elections KPP joined the All India Trinamool Congress-led Bangla Bachao Front.

In spring 2003 KPP suffered an internal division. Atul Roy, considered as a moderate, was dethroned and replaced by a more hardline leadership. The present president of KPP is Nikhil Roy and the general secretary is Subhas Burman. Atul Roy remains a member of the central committee.

Ahead of the 2004 Lok Sabha elections KPP formed a front together with Jharkhand Mukti Morcha.

Madhyamik Teachers' Sangh

Madhyamik Teachers' Sangh, a movement of teachers in the Indian state of West Bengal. MTS is the teachers wing of All India Forward Bloc.

Marxist Forward Bloc

Marxist Forward Bloc, is a splinter-group of All India Forward Bloc. MFB was formed in 1953 as Satyapria Banerjee, a member of the AIFB Central Secretariat, Amar Bose, Suhurit Chaudhury and Ram Chatterji were expelled from AIFB. At its foundation, Satyapria Banerji was the party general secretary and Amar Bose its chairman.

MFB has been associated with the combined left movement since its inception. Its leader Ram Chatterjee was a minister in the Bengal Left Front Government for several years. Today MFB is led by Pratim Chatterjee, Fire services minister of West Bengal. Chatterjee represents Tarakeswar. MFB is part of the Left Front.

In West Bengal assembly elections MFB contests Tarakeswar and Jamalpur seats as a Left Front partner. In the 2006 West Bengal legislative assembly election, the party retained both seats. In the Kolkata municipal polls in 2005, MFB contested in 2 wards as a Left Front partner. Biren Chakroborty who is the secretary of MFB was elected from ward no 57.

Party of Democratic Socialism (India)

The Party of Democratic Socialism (PDS) is a political party in West Bengal in India. The PDS was founded in February 2001 by expelled Communist Party of India (Marxist) (CPI(M)) leader Saifuddin Chaudhury. The PDS is in opposition to the Left Front government in West Bengal, and they have aligned themselves with the Indian National Congress.

Initially there was speculation that the PDS would joint with the All India Trinamool Congress, or else that it would be a constituent of an anti-CPI(M) *mahajot* (broad front), but the link between Trinamool and the Hindu rightist BJP hindered such a development.

The PDS has formed relations with other pro-Congress leftist outfits, such as the Communist Marxist Party in Kerala and the United Communist Party of India.

Ahead of the West Bengal state assembly elections in 2001, the PDS had launched their own front. The PDS put up 98 candidates, who together got 219,082 votes (0.6% of the votes in the state). None of their candidates were elected.

Ahead of the Lok Sabha elections in 2004, the PDS had joined hands with Congress, and put up two candidates supported by Congress.

The flag of the PDS is a red flag with a red star in a white circle.

The president of the PDS is Saifuddin Chaudhury, the general secretary is Samir Putatunda (formerly the CPI(M) South 24 Paraganas district secretary), and the treasurer is Subir Chaudhury.

The women's organization of the PDS is called *Paschim Banga Nari Sanghati Samiti* (West Bengal Women's United Association). The president of PBNSS is Kishwar Jahan.

The PDS publishes *Amader Katha* (Our Voice).

Paschimbanga Ganatantrik Manch

Paschimbanga Ganatantrik Manch (West Bengal Democratic Platform) is a political party in the Indian state of West Bengal. PGM was formed in 1999 by expelled members of Communist Party of India (Marxist). The convenor of PGM is Sumanta Hira, former member of the Legislative Assembly of West Bengal for CPI(M).

In the 2001 state assembly elections Hira stood as the only PGM candidate, contesting the Taltola seat. He got 551 votes (0.7%).

WEST BENGAL LEGISLATIVE ASSEMBLY

The West Bengal Legislative Assembly — the Vidhan Sabha is the unicameral legislature of the Indian state of West Bengal. It is situated in the B.B.D. Bagh area of Kolkata (Kolkata) — the capotal of the state. Members of the Legislative assembly are directly elected by the people. The assembly consists of 295 MLA including one nominated from the Anglo-Indian community. Its term is 5 years, unless sooner dissolved.

4

Language and Literature

BENGALI LANGUAGE

Bengali , also known by its endonym Bangla, is an Indo-Aryan language primarily spoken by the Bengalis in the Indian subcontinent. It is the official and most widely spoken language of Bangladesh and second most widely spoken of the 22 scheduled languages of India, behind Hindi.

The official and *de facto* national language of Bangladesh is Modern Standard Bengali (Literary Bengali). It serves as the *lingua franca* of the nation, with 98% of Bangladeshis being fluent in Bengali (including dialects) as their first language. Within India, Bengali is the official language of the states of West Bengal, Tripura and the Barak Valley in the state of Assam. It is also spoken in different parts of the Brahmaputra valley of Assam. It is also the most widely spoken language in the Andaman and Nicobar Islands in the Bay of Bengal, and is spoken by significant minorities in other states including Jharkhand, Bihar, Mizoram, Meghalaya, and Odisha. With approximately 250–300 million total speakers worldwide, Bengali is usually counted as the seventh most spoken native language in the world by population.

Dictionaries from the early 20th century attributed slightly more than half of the Bengali vocabulary to native words (i.e., naturally modified Sanskrit words, corrupted forms of Sanskrit words, and loanwords from non-Indo-European languages), about 30 percent to unmodified Sanskrit words, and the remainder to foreign words.

Dominant in the last group was Persian, which was also the source of some grammatical forms. More recent studies suggest that the use of native and foreign words has been increasing, mainly because of the preference of Bengali speakers for the colloquial style.

Bengali literature, with its millennium-old history and folk heritage, has extensively developed since the Bengali renaissance and is one of the most prominent and diverse literary traditions in Asia.

Both the national anthems of Bangladesh (*Amar Sonar Bangla*) and India (*Jana Gana Mana*) were composed in Bengali by Rabindranath Tagore.

The first two verses of a patriotic song written in Bengali by Bankim Chandra Chatterjee, *Vande Mataram*, was adopted as the "national song" of India in both the colonial period and later in 1950 in independent India.

Furthermore, it is believed by many that the national anthem of Sri Lanka (Sri Lanka Matha) was inspired by a Bengali poem written by Rabindranath Tagore, while some even believe the anthem was originally written in Bengali and then translated into Sinhalese.

In 1952, the Bengali Language Movement successfully pushed for the language's official status in the Dominion of Pakistan, allowing for education in and official use of the language.

In 1999, UNESCO recognized 21 February as International Mother Language Day in recognition of the language movement in East Bengal (now Bangladesh). Language is an important element of Bengali identity and binds together a culturally diverse region.

History

Silver coin with proto-Bengali script, Harikela Kingdom, circa 9th-13th century

Ancient language of Bengal

Sanskrit was spoken in Bengal since the first millennium BCE. During the Gupta Empire, Bengal was a hub of Sanskrit literature.

The Middle Indo-Aryan dialects were spoken in Bengal in the first millennium when the region was a part of the Magadha Realm. These dialects were called Magadhi Prakrit.

Middle Bengali

During the medieval period, Middle Bengali was characterized by the elision of word-final, the spread of compound verbs and Arabic and Persian influences.

Bengali was an official court language of the Sultanate of Bengal. Muslim rulers promoted the literary development of Bengali.

Bengali became the most spoken vernacular language in the Sultanate. This period saw borrowing of Perso-Arabic terms into Bengali vocabulary. Major texts of Middle Bengali (1400–1800) include Chandidas' *Shreekrishna Kirtana.*

Modern Bengali

The modern literary form of Bengali was developed during the 19th and early 20th centuries based on the dialect spoken in the Nadia region, a west-central Bengali dialect. Bengali presents a strong case of diglossia, with the literary and standard form differing greatly from the colloquial speech of the regions that identify with the language. The modern Bengali vocabularycontains the vocabulary base from Magadhi Prakrit and Pali, also tatsamas and reborrowings from Sanskrit and other major borrowings from Persian, Arabic, Austroasiatic languages and other languages in contact with.

The Central Shaheed Minar in Dhaka commemorates the Bengali Language Movement. UNESCOcommemorates the movement as International Mother Language Day.

During this period, the

- *Chôlitôbhasha* form of Bengali using simplified inflections and other changes, was emerging from
- *Sadhubhasha* (Proper form or original form of Bengali) as the form of choice for written Bengali.

In 1948 the Government of Pakistan tried to impose Urdu as the sole state language in Pakistan, starting the Bengali language movement. The Bengali Language Movement was a popular ethno-linguistic movement in the former East Bengal (today Bangladesh), which was a result of the strong linguistic consciousness of the Bengalis to gain and protect spoken and written Bengali's recognition as a state language of the then Dominion of Pakistan. On the day of 21 February 1952 five students and political activists were killed during protests near the campus of the University of Dhaka.

In 1956 Bengali was made a state language of Pakistan. The day has since been observed as Language Movement Day in Bangladesh and was proclaimed International Mother Language Day by UNESCO on 17 November 1999.

This gives Bengali the distinction of being the only language in the world that is known for its language movements and people sacrificing their lives for its preservation.

A Bengali language movement in the Indian state of Assam took place in 1961, a protest against the decision of the Government of Assam to make Assamese the only official language of the state even though a significant proportion of the population were Bengali-speaking, particularly in the Barak Valley.

In 2010, the parliament of Bangladesh and the legislative assembly of West Bengal proposed that Bengali be made an official UN language. Their motions came after Bangladeshi Prime Minister Sheikh Hasina suggested the idea while addressing the UN General Assembly that year.

Geographical distribution

Bengali language is native to the region of Bengal, which comprises Indian states of West Bengal and the present-day nation of Bangladesh.

Besides the native region it is also spoken by the Bengalis living in Tripura, southern Assam and the Bengali population in the Indian union territory of Andaman and Nicobar Islands. Bengali is also spoken in the neighboring states of Odisha, Bihar, and Jharkhand, and sizable minorities of Bengali speakers reside in Indian cities outside Bengal, including Delhi, Mumbai, Varanasi, and Vrindavan.

There are also significant Bengali-speaking communities in the Middle East, the United States, Singapore, Malaysia, Australia, Canada and the United Kingdom and Italy.

Official status

Bengali is national and official language of Bangladesh, and one of the 23 official languages in India. It is the official language of the Indian states of West Bengal, Tripura and in Barak Valley of Assam. Bengali is a second official language of the Indian state of Jharkhand since September 2011. It is also a recognized secondary language in the City of Karachi in Pakistan. The Department of Bengali in the University of Karachi also offers regular programs of studies at the Bachelors and at the Masters levels for Bengali Literature.

The national anthems of both Bangladesh and India were written in Bengali by the Bengali Nobel laureate Rabindranath Tagore. In 2009, elected representatives in both Bangladesh and West Bengal called for Bengali language to be made an official language of the United Nations.

Spoken and literary varieties

Bengali exhibits diglossia, though some scholars have proposed triglossia or even n-glossia or heteroglossia between the written and spoken forms of the language.Two styles of writing have emerged, involving somewhat different vocabularies and syntax:

1. *Shadhu-bhasha* was the written language, with longer verb inflections and more of a Pali and Sanskrit-derived *Tatsama* vocabulary. Songs such as India's national anthem *Jana Gana Mana* (by Rabindranath Tagore) were composed in Shadhubhasha. However, use of Shadhubhasha in modern writing is uncommon, restricted to some official signs and documents in Bangladesh as well as for achieving particular literary effects.
2. *Cholito-bhasha* , known by linguists as Standard Colloquial Bengali, is a written Bengali style exhibiting a preponderance of colloquial idiom and shortened verb forms, and is the standard for written Bengali now. This form came into vogue towards the turn of the 19th century, promoted by the writings of Peary Chand Mitra (*Alaler*

Gharer Dulal, 1857), Pramatha Chaudhuri (*Sabujpatra*, 1914) and in the later writings of Rabindranath Tagore. It is modeled on the dialect spoken in the Shantipur region in Nadia district, West Bengal. This form of Bengali is often referred to as the "Nadia standard", "Nadia dialect", "Southwestern/West-Central dialect" or "Shantipuri Bangla".

Linguist Prabhat Ranjan Sarkar, categorizes the language as:

- Madhya Râdhi dialect
- Kanthi (Contai) dialect
- Kolkata dialect
- Shantipuri (Nadia) dialect
- Maldahiya (Jangipuri) dialect
- Barendri dialect
- Rangpuriya dialect
- Sylheti dialect
- Dhakaiya (Bikrampuri) dialect
- Jessor/ Jessoriya dialect
- Barisal (Chandradwip) dialect
- Chattal (Chittagong) dialect

While most writing is in Standard Colloquial Bengali (SCB), spoken dialects exhibit a greater variety. People in southeastern West Bengal, including Kolkata, speak in SCB. Other dialects, with minor variations from Standard Colloquial, are used in other parts of West Bengal and western Bangladesh, such as the Midnapore dialect, characterised by some unique words and constructions. However, a majority in Bangladesh speak in dialects notably different from SCB. Some dialects, particularly those of the Chittagong region, bear only a superficial resemblance to SCB. The dialect in the Chittagong region is least widely understood by the general body of Bengalis. The majority of Bengalis are able to communicate in more than one variety—often, speakers are fluent in *Cholitobhasha* (SCB) and one or more regional dialects.

LITERATURE

Rabindranath Tagore is Asia's first Nobel laureateand the composer of India's national anthem.

Swami Vivekananda was a key figure in introducing Vedanta and Yoga to Europe and the US,raising interfaith awareness and making Hinduism a world religion.

The Bengali language boasts a rich literary heritage that it shares with neighbouring Bangladesh. West Bengal has a long tradition of folk literature, evidenced by the *Charyapada*, a collection of Buddhist mystic songs dating back to the 10th and 11th centuries; *Mangalkavya*, a collection of Hindu narrative poetry composed around the 13th century; *Shreekrishna Kirtana*, a pastoral Vaishnava drama in verse composed by Boru Chandidas; *Thakurmar Jhuli*, a collection of Bengali folk and fairy tales compiled by Dakshinaranjan Mitra Majumder; and stories of Gopal Bhar, a court jester in medieval Bengal. In the 19th and 20th centuries, Bengali literature was modernised in the works of authors such as Bankim Chandra Chattopadhyay, whose innovative works marked a departure from the traditional verse-oriented writings prevalent in that period; Michael Madhusudan Dutt, a pioneer in Bengali drama who introduced the use of blank verse; and Rabindranath Tagore, who reshaped Bengali literature and music. Indian art saw the introduction of Contextual Modernism in the late 19th and early 20th centuries. Other notable figures include Kazi Nazrul Islam, whose compositions form the avant-garde genre of *Nazrul Sangeet*, Sarat Chandra Chattopadhyay, whose works on contemporary social practices in Bengal are widely acclaimed, and Manik Bandyopadhyay, who is considered one of the leading lights of modern Bengali fiction. In modern times, Jibanananda Das has been acknowledged as "the premier poet of the post-Tagore era in India". Other writers include Bibhutibhushan Bandopadhyay, best known for his work *Pather Panchali*; Tarashankar Bandopadhyay, well known for his portrayal of the lower strata of society; Manik Bandopadhyay, a pioneering novelist; and Ashapurna Devi, Shirshendu Mukhopadhyay, Saradindu Bandopadhyay, Buddhadeb Guha, Mahashweta Devi, Samaresh Majumdar, Sanjeev Chattopadhyay, Shakti Chattopadhyay, Buddhadeb Basu, Joy Goswami, and Sunil Gangopadhyay.

BENGALI LITERATURE

The first evidence of Bengali literature is known as Charyapada or Charyageeti, which were Buddhist hymns from the 8th century. Charyapada is in the oldest known written form of Bengali. The famous Bengali linguist Harprashad Shastri discovered the palm leaf Charyapada manuscript in the Nepal Royal Court Library in 1907.

Starting of Modern Era: In the middle of 19th century, Bengali literature gained momentum. During this period, the Bengali *Pandits* of Fort William College did the tedious work of translating the text books in Bengali to help teach the British some Indian languages including Bengali. This work played a role in the background in the evolution of Bengali prose.

Raja Ram Mohan Roy: Raja Ram Mohan Roy arrived in Kolkata in 1814 and engaged in literary pursuits. Translating from Sanskrit to Bengali, writing essays on religious topics and publishing magazines were some the areas he focussed on. He established a cultural group in the name of 'Atyio Sova' (Club of Kins) in 1815.

Ishwar Chandra Vidyasagar: Ishwar Chandra Bandyopadhyaya (popularly known as "Vidyasagar" which means 'ocean of knowledge') was mainly known as a social reformer and an educator. But his contribution to the Bengali literature was also crucially important. Most modern scholars agree that, it was he who played the most significant role in the inception of effective Bengali prose writing, partly laying the foundation of modern Bengali literature.

Vidysagar realized the need of educating women in the society. With his tireless effort to uplift the status of women in the society, he was able to establish some Girl's schools in different parts of Bengal. But there was no good Bengali text book for basic Bengali education. He wrote Bengali books with basic language construct and fundamentals, like, "Barnaparichay", "Bodhoday", "Kathamala", etc. and then easy grammar books like "Upakramonika" and "Byakaron Kaumudi".

He also introduced some basic books for Mathematical logic. Rabindranath Tagore called him as the father of modern Bengali language. Vidyasagar translated some masterpieces of Sanskrit and English literature into Bengali: "betaal panchabingshati" (Sanskrit Kathasarit sagar, "shakuntala", "bhranti bilaas", "sitaar banabaas" and edited books like "raghubangsha", "kumarsambhab", etc.

Parichand Mitra: Parichand Mitra (penname Tekchand Thakur), is widely considered to be the first Bengali novelist for his novel "Alaler Ghore Dulal". This novel was published in 1858. In this novel he used the colloquial language, something that was almost unthinkable for the literati of his time.

Impact of Nil Bidroho and Dinabandhu Mitra: In 1857, the famous 'Sipahi Biplob' (Sepoy Mutiny) took place. With the wind of it, 'Nil Bidroho' (Blue Revolt) scattered all over then Bengal region. This Nil Bidroho lasted for more than a year (In 1859-1860). The literature world was shaken with this revolt. In the light of this revolt, a great drama was published from Dhaka in the name of 'Nil Dorpon' (The Blue Mirror). Dinabandhu Mitra was the writer of this play.

Michael Madhusudan Dutt: In this time, Michael Madhusudan Dutt emerged as the first epic-poet of modern bangla literature. Dutt, a Christian by conversion, is best known for his Ramayana-based masterpiece, "The Slaying of Meghnadh," which essentially follows in the poetic tradition of Milton's *Paradise Lost*. Those who have read it consider this work a world-class epic poem of the modern era. Michael Madhusudan Dutta is also credited with the introduction of sonnets to Bangla literature. He ruled the bangla literature world for more than a decade (1858-1863).

Bankim Chandra Chattopadhyay: Bankim Chandra Chattopadhyay starts his journey through bangla literature with his first published novel 'Durgeshnondini' (Daughter of the Fort Lord) in 1865. He is considered as one of the leading Bengali novelists and is popularly known as the author of India's first *national song*, "Bande Matarom" (pronounced in Hindi "Vande Mataram").

Others: Bangla literature also become rich with its variations. It started to spread its different branches also in poetry Ishwar Chandra Vidyasagar, Biharilal Chokroborty, Kaykobad, in novel Romeshchandra Dutt, Mir Mosharraf Hossain, in plays Girish Chandra Gosh, in essays Akshay Kumar Boral, Ramendro Sundar Tribedy and many others contributed to enrich bangla literature in this time. A lot of literature magazines and newspapers started to come under day light. A number of educational institutes appears all over the region. This helps a lot to nurture the future author and poets of bangla language.

Influence of Rabindranath Tagore: Possibly the most prolific writer in Bangla is Nobel laureate Rabindranath Tagore. Tagore dominated both the Bengali and Indian philosophical and literary scene for decades. His 2,000 *Rabindrasangeets* play a pivotal part in defining Bengali culture, both in West Bengal and Bangladesh. He is the author of the national anthems of both India and Bangladesh, both composed in Bangla.

Other notable Bangla works of his are *Gitanjali*, a book of poems for which he was awarded the Nobel Prize for Literature in 1913, and many short stories and a few novels. It is widely accepted that Bangla Literature accomplished its contemporary look by the writings and influence of Rabindranath.

Kazi Nazrul Islam: In a similar category is Kazi Nazrul Islam, a Muslim who was invited to post-partition Bangladesh as the National Poet and whose work transcends sectarian boundaries. Adored by Bengalis both in Bangladesh and West Bengal, his work includes 3,000 songs, known as both as *nazrul geeti* and "nazrul sangeet". He is frequently called the rebel poet mainly because of his most famous and electrifying poem "Bidrohi" or "The Rebel", and also because of his strong sympathy and support for revolutionary activities leading to India's independence from British Rule. His songs and poems were frequently used during the Bangladesh Liberation War as well. Though he is acknowledged as the rebel poet, Nazrul very effectively contributed in all branches of literature. He wrote poems that lights the fire against enequality or unjust and the same time he wrote some awesome romantic poems. He wrote a lot of Islami Gazals and in the same time wrote a number of *Shyama Sangeet* (songs for the Hindu Mother Goddess, Kali). Nazrul was not only a poet, he was writer, musician, journalist and philosopher. He was sent to jail for his literary works against then prevailing British rule.

Bengali Literature

Bengal has always been a major center of art, culture and literature in India. The soil of Bengal has given intellectuals like Rabindra Nath Tagore, Raja Ram Roy, Kazi Nazrul Islam, Bankim Chandra and Ishwar Chandra Vidyasagar to the world of literature. The term 'Bengali literature' includes all the literary work in Bengali language, be it from Bangladesh or West Bengal. Bengali literature is one of the oldest available literatures in the world, as its history can be traced to centuries ago. Like Bengali music, Bengali literature is also very rich and relevant.

The first available evidence of the ancient Bengali literature comprises of a collection of 8th-12th century Buddhist spiritualist poems, from Eastern India, called Charyapada or Charyageeti. The poets of these Charyapadas were the Siddhas or Siddhacharyas, who belonged to the states of Assam, Bengal, Orissa and Bihar. These texts also make up the oldest written form of Bengali language, available in the present times. Charyapada was discovered by Bengali linguist Harprashad Shastri, written on palm leaves, in the Nepal Royal Court Library, in 1907.

Bengali literature gained momentum in 19th century, when great laureates like Raja Ram Mohan Roy and Vidyasagar started actively participating and working towards its development. In the later half of 19th century, the focus came on novel-writing. The first Bengali novel was Peary Chandra Mitra's Alaler Ghorer Dulal, which came out in 1858. The other popular novels in that era were Durgesh-Nandini, Debdas, Premer Somadhi, Goriber Meye, Premer Pothe, Nodibakshe and Abdullah.

In the later half of 19th century, Bengali poetry, plays and contemporary media also flourished. Rabindra Nath Tagore, Bihari Lal Chkrobarty, Saradamangal and Sadhar Asan brought freshness to Bengali poetry wing. Periodical press, with Digdarshan and Samachar-Darpan, also gained momentum. In this phase, the developing Bengali literature greatly contributed to Indian freedom struggle as well. By 20th century, the rendezvous of Bengal with Renaissance brought about a revolution of socialist reforms, through contemporary literature.

Even today, Bengali literature stands as an important section of Indian Literature. A major chunk of Bengali population still prefers the rich regional literature relevant to their society, in comparison to the foreign literatures. Some of the famous names in contemporary Bengali literature are Sunil Gangopadhyaya, Buddhadev Guha, Mahashweta Devi, Samaresh Majumdar, Amiya Bhushan Majumdar,Sankha Ghosh, Debesh Roy, Bani Basu, Malay Roy and Moti Nandi. Many famous Bollywood movies, like Parineeta and Devdas, have had their scripts adapted from famous Bengali novels only.

Other Notable

Novelists: Sarat Chandra Chattopadhyay was one of the most popular novelists of early 20th century whose speciality was exploring complex human psychology and drama. Tarashankar Bandopadhay was another famous novelist whose works feature a realistic picture of the many-coloured fabric of life in rural Bengal in a pioneering modernist style of prose in fiction.

Other famous bengali novelists are Bibhuti Bhushan Bandopadhyay, Manik Bandopadhyay, Balai Chand Mukhopadhyay (Banophool), Saradindu Bandopadhyay, Bimal Mitra, Bimal Kar, Samaresh Basu, etc. Early bengali science fiction works were also written in the 19th and early 20th centuries by writers such as Jagadananda Roy, Hemlal Dutta, Jagdish Chandra Bose, Premendra Mitra, Satyajit Ray, etc.

Short Story Writers: Bengali literature is also famous for short stories. Some of the famous short story writers are Rabindranath Tagore, Manik Bandopadhyay, Tarashankar, Bibhuti Bhushan Bandopadhyay, Raj Shekhar Basu (Parasuram), Premendra Mitra, Sibram Chakraborty, Saradindu Bandopadhyay, Subodh Ghosh, Narendra Nath Mitra,

Narayan Gangopadhyay, Santosh Ghosh, etc.

The famous Bengali film director Satyajit Ray also wrote many short stories. One of his stories was *Bankubabur Bandhu* (*Banku Babu's Friend*) written in 1962, which was the first science fiction story to portray an alien from outer space as a benign and playful being invested with magical powers and best capable of interacting with children, in contrast to earlier science fiction stories which portrayed aliens as dangerous monsters. He later adapted the story as a script for a film called *The Alien* in 1967, though the film was later cancelled. However, Ray's story was strikingly similar to Spielberg's film *E.T.* later released in 1982, which may have been inspired by Ray's script for *The Alien.*

Poets: Jibanananda Das was a famous poet who, along with Buddhadev Basu, marks the beginning of the move to transcend the Tagore legacy. The new genere of Bengali poets departed considerably from Tagore's ideological style and adopted realism in their writing more pronouncedly. Titled **polli-kobi** (*Poet of the Village*) for works relating to the villages and countryside of Bengal, Jasimuddin is particularly famous for his poems that have become major highlights for pedagogical purposes in both West Bengal and Bangladesh. Shamsur Rahman is widely known for his 'playing with words'. *He has built on the ground of the 30's poets, but he has developed the ground, explored into areas they thought too dark for exploration, has added new features to it, landscaped it and in the process left his footprints all over.*

Musicians: Seminal Hindu religious works in Bangla include the many songs of Ramprasad Sen. His works (still sung today) from the 17th century cover an astonishing range of emotional responses to the goddess Kali, detailing complex philosophical statements based on Vedanta teachings and more visceral prouncements of his love of the goddess. They are known as *Shyama Sangeet* and were the literary inspiration for Kazi Nazrul Islam's later, famed Shyama Sangeet. There are also the laudatory accounts of the lives and teachings of the Vaishnava saint Chaitanya Mahaprabhu (the *Choitanyo*

Choritamrit) and Shri Ramakrishna (the *Ramakrishna Kathamrita*, translated roughly as Gospel of Ramakrishna). There is also a large body of Islamic literature, that can be traced back at least to *Noornama* by Abdul Hakim. *Bishad Sindhu* depicting the death of Hussain in Karbala is very popular novel written by Mir Mosharraf Hussain. Later works influenced by Islam include devotional songs written by Nazrul, and popularized by Abbas-ud-din, among others.

Bauls and Traditional Singers: The mystic Bauls of the Bengal countryside who preached the boundless spiritual truth of *Sohoj Poth* (the Simple, Natural Path) and *Moner Manush* (The Man of The Heart) drew on Vedantic philosophy to propound transcendental truths in song format, travelling from village to village proclaiming that there was no such thing as Hindu, Muslim or Christian, only *moner manush*.

The literature discussed so far can be more or less regarded as the common heritage of both Bangladesh and West Bengal. Since the partition of Bengal in 1947, the east and west parts of Bengal have also developed their own distinctive literatures. For example, the Naxalite movement has influenced much of West Bengal's literature, whereas the Liberation War has had a similarly profound impact on Bangladeshi literature.

Major literary figures in Bangladesh include Shamsur Rahman, Sufia Kamal, Hasan Azizul Huq, Akhtaruzzaman Ilias and Humayun Azad, to name a few. Some notable writers from West Bengal are Sunil Gangopadhyay, Shankha Ghosh, Shakti Chattopadhyay, Mahasweta Devi and Joy Goswami.

5

Geography and Flora & Fauna

GEOGRAPHIC OVERVIEW

Tribal peoples constitute 8.3% of the nation's total population, over 84 million people according to the 2001 census. One concentration lives in a belt along the Himalayas stretching through Jammu and Kashmir, Himachal Pradesh, and Uttarakhand in the west, to Assam, Meghalaya, Tripura, Arunachal Pradesh, Mizoram, Manipur, and Nagaland in the northeast. In the northeastern states of Arunachal Pradesh, Meghalaya, Mizoram, and Nagaland, upward of 90% of the population is tribal. However, in the remaining northeast states of Assam, Manipur, Sikkim, and Tripura, tribal peoples form between 20 and 30% of the population.

Another concentration lives in the hilly areas of central India (Chhattisgarh, Madhya Pradesh, Orissa, and, to a lesser extent, Andhra Pradesh); in this belt, which is bounded by the Narmada River to the north and the Godavari River to the southeast, tribal peoples occupy the slopes of the region's mountains. Other tribals, including the Santals, live in Jharkhand and West Bengal. Central Indian states have the country's largest tribes, and, taken as a whole, roughly 75 % of the total tribal population live there, although the tribal population there accounts for only around 10% of the region's total population.

There are smaller numbers of tribal people in Karnataka, Tamil Nadu, and Kerala in south India; in western India in Gujarat and Rajasthan, and in the union territories of Lakshadweep and the Andaman Islands and Nicobar Islands. About one percent of the populations of Kerala and Tamil Nadu are tribal, whereas about six percent in Andhra Pradesh and Karnataka are members of tribes.

CRITERIA OF 'TRIBALNESS'

Apart from the use of strictly legal criteria, however, the problem of determining which groups and individuals are tribal is both subtle and complex. Because it concerns economic interests and voting blocs, the question of who are members of Scheduled Tribes rather than Backward Classes or Scheduled Castes is often controversial.

A number of traits have customarily been seen as establishing tribal rather than caste identity. These include language, social organization, religious affiliation, economic patterns, geographic location, and self-identification. Recognized tribes typically live in hilly regions somewhat remote from caste settlements; they generally speak a language recognized as tribal.

Unlike castes, which form part of a complex and interrelated local economic exchange system, tribes tend to form self-sufficient economic units. For most tribal people, land-use rights traditionally derive simply from tribal membership. Tribal society tends to the egalitarian, with its leadership based on ties of kinship and personality rather than on hereditary status. Tribes typically consist of segmentary lineages whose extended families provide the basis for social organization and control. Tribal religion recognizes no authority outside the tribe.

Any of these criteria may not apply in specific instances. Language does not always give an accurate indicator of tribal or caste status. Especially in regions of mixed population, many tribal groups have lost their mother tongues and simply speak local or regional languages. In parts of Assam - an area historically divided between warring tribes and villages - increased contact among villagers began during the colonial period, and has accelerated since independence in 1947. A pidgin Assamese developed while educated tribal members learned Hindi and, in the late twentieth century, English.

Self-identification and group loyalty do not provide unfailing markers of tribal identity either. In the case of stratified tribes, the loyalties of clan, kin, and family may well predominate over those of tribe. In addition, tribes cannot always be viewed as people living apart; the degree of isolation of various tribes has varied tremendously. The Gonds, Santals, and Bhils traditionally have dominated the regions in which they have lived. Moreover, tribal society is not always more egalitarian than the rest of the rural populace; some of the larger tribes, such as the Gonds, are highly stratified.

The apparently wide fluctuation in estimates of South Asia's tribal population through the twentieth century gives a sense of how unclear the distinction between tribal and nontribal can be. India's 1931 census enumerated 22 million tribal people, in 1941 only 10 million were counted, but by 1961 some 30 million and in 1991 nearly 68 million tribal members were included. The differences among the figures reflect changing census criteria and the economic incentives individuals have to maintain or reject classification as a tribal member.

These gyrations of census data serve to underline the complex relationship between caste and tribe. Although, in theory, these terms represent different ways of life and ideal types, in reality they stand for a continuum of social groups. In areas of substantial contact between tribes and castes, social and cultural pressures have often tended to move tribes in the direction of becoming castes over a period of years.

Tribal peoples with ambitions for social advancement in Indian society at large have tried to gain the classification of caste for their tribes. On occasion, an entire tribe or part of a tribe joined a Hindu sect and thus entered the caste system *en masse*. If a specific tribe engaged in practices that Hindus deemed polluting, the tribe's status when it was assimilated into the caste hierarchy would be affected.

Since independence, however, the special benefits available to Scheduled Tribes have convinced many groups, even Hindus and Muslims, that they will enjoy greater advantages if so designated. The schedule gives tribal people incentives to maintain their identity. By the same token, the schedule also includes a number of groups whose 'tribal' status, in cultural terms, is dubious at best.

GEOGRAPHY OF BENGAL

Geography of West Bengal is full of variety. It consists of high peaks of Himalaya in the northern extremes to coastal regions down south, with regions like plateu, Ganges delta etc. intervening in between. It may be interesting to note that West Bengal is only state in India where Himalayas are in the north and Sea is at the south, with both plaines and plateau are covering the remaining region.

West Bengal is on the eastern bottleneck of India, stretching from the Himalayas in the north to the Bay of Bengal in the south. The state has a total area of 88,752 square kilometres (34,267 mi²). The Darjeeling Himalayan hill region in the northern extreme of the state belongs to the eastern Himalaya. This region contains Sandakfu (3,636 metres (11,929 ft.))—the highest peak of the state. The narrow Terai region separates this region from the plains, which in turn transitions into the Ganges delta towards the south. The Rarh region intervenes between the Ganges delta in the east and the western plateau and high lands. A small coastal region is on the extreme south, while the Sundarbans mangrove forests form a remarkable geographical landmark at the Ganges delta.

The Ganges is the main river, which divides in West Bengal. One branch enters Bangladesh as the *Padma* or *Podda*, while the other flows through West Bengal as the Bhagirathi River and Hooghly River. The Teesta, Torsa, Jaldhaka and Mahananda rivers are in the northern hilly region. The western plateau region has rivers such as the Damodar, Ajay and Kangsabati.

The Ganges delta and the Sundarbans area have numerous rivers and creeks. Pollution of the Ganges from indiscriminate waste dumped into the river is a major problem. At least nine districts in the state suffer from arsenic contamination of groundwater, and an estimated 8.7 million people drink water containing arsenic above the World Health Organisation recommended limit of 10 μg/L.

West Bengal's climate varies from tropical savannah in the southern portions to humid subtropical in the north. The main seasons are summer, rainy season, a short autumn, and winter. While the summer in the delta region is noted for excessive humidity, the western highlands experience a dry summer like northern India, with the highest day temperature ranging from 38 °C (100 °F) to 45 °C (113 °F).

At nights, a cool southerly breeze carries moisture from the Bay of Bengal. In early summer brief squalls and thunderstorms known as *Kalbaisakhi*, or Nor'westers, often occur. Monsoons bring rain to the whole state from June to September. West Bengal receives the Bay of Bengal branch of the Indian ocean monsoon that moves in a northwest direction. Winter (December–January) is mild over the plains with average minimum temperatures of 15 °C (59 °F). A cold and dry northern wind blows in the winter, substantially lowering the humidity level. However, the Darjeeling Himalayan Hill region experiences a harsh winter, with occasional snowfall at places.

FLORA AND FAUNA

Owing to the varying altitude from the Himalayas to the coastal plains, the flora and fauna of the state is diverse. Forests make up 14% of the geographical area of West Bengal, which is lower than the national average of 23%. Protected forests cover 4% of the state area. Part of the world's largest mangrove forest Sundarbans is located in southern West Bengal.

From a phytogeographic viewpoint, the southern part of West Bengal can be divided into two regions: the Gangetic plain and the littoral mangrove forests of the Sundarbans. The alluvial soil of the Gangetic plain compounded with favourable rainfall make this region especially fertile. Much of the vegetation of the western part of the state shares floristic similarities with the plants of the Chota Nagpur plateau in the adjoining state of Jharkhand.

The predominant commercial tree species is *Shorea robusta,* commonly known as Sal. The coastal region of Purba Medinipur exhibits coastal vegetation; the predominant tree is the *Casuarina.* The most valuable tree from the Sundarbans is the ubiquitous *sundri* (*Heritiera fomes*) from which the forest gets its name. Vegetation in northern West Bengal is dictated by elevation and precipitation. For example, the foothills of the Himalayas, the *Dooars,* are densely wooded with Sal and other trees of the tropical evergreen type. Above 1000 m, the forest type changes to subtropical. In Darjeeling, which is above 1500 m, common trees typifying the temperate forest are oaks, conifers, and rhododendrons.

The Sundarbans are noted for a reserve project conserving Bengal tigers. There are five national parks in the state—Sundarbans National Park, Buxa Tiger Reserve, Gorumara National Park, Neora Valley National Park and Singalila National Park. Wildlife includes the Indian rhinoceros, Indian elephants, deer, bison, leopards, gaur, and crocodiles. The state is also rich in bird life. Migratory birds come to the state during the winter. The high altitude forests like Singalila National Park shelter barking deer, red panda, chinkara, takin, serow, pangolin, minivet and Kalij pheasants. In addition to the Bengal tiger, the Sundarbans host many other endangered species like the Ganges River Dolphin, river terrapin, estuarine crocodile etc. The mangrove forest also acts as a natural fish nursery, supporting coastal fishes along the Bay of Bengal.

Demographics: The vast majority of the 80,221,171 people of West Bengal are Bengalis. Bihari minority is scattered throughout the state and communites of Sherpas and ethnic Tibetans can be found in regions bordering Sikkim. West Bengal is also home to indigenous tribal *Adivasis* (including Santals and Kol), who are mostly concentrated in the western districts.

The official language is Bengali. Hindi and English are also used commonly. Nepali is spoken primarily by the Gorkhas of Darjeeling district. Hinduism is the principal religion - 72.5% of the population are Hindus. Muslims comprise 25%, and other religions make up the remainder.

West Bengal has a population density of 904 people/km^2 making it the most densely populated state in India. The state contributes 7.81% of India's population. The state's 1991–2001 growth rate of 17.84% is slightly lower than the national rate of 21.34%. The gender ratio is 934 females per 1000 males.

The literacy rate is 69.22%. The life expectancy in the state is 63.4 years, marginally higher than the national value of 61.7 years. About 72% of people live in rural areas. The proportion of people living below the poverty line in 1999-2000 was 31.85%. Scheduled Castes and Tribes form 28.6% and 5.8% of the population respectively in rural areas, and 19.9% and 1.5% respectively in urban areas.

The crime rate in the state in 2004 was 82.6 per 100,000, which was half of the national average. This is the fourth-lowest crime rate among the 32 states and union territories of India. However, the state reported the highest rate of Special and Local Laws (SLL) crimes. In reported crimes against women, the state showed a crime rate of 7.1 compared to the national rate of 14.1. West Bengal was the first Indian state to constitute a Human Rights Commission of its own.

CITIES

Kolkata

Kolkata (formerly Calcutta)) is the capital of the Indian state of West Bengal. It is located in eastern India on the east bank of the River Hooghly. The city has a population of almost 6 million, with an extended metropolitan population of over 14 million, making it the third-largest urban agglomeration and the fourth-largest city in India.

The city served as the capital of India during the British Raj until 1911. Once the centre of modern education, science, culture and politics in India, Kolkata witnessed economic stagnation in the years following India's independence in 1947. However, since the year 2000 an economic rejuvenation has arrested the morbid decline, leading to a spurt in the city's growth. Like other large cities, Kolkata continues to struggle with urbanisation problems like poverty, pollution and traffic congestion.

A vibrant city with a distinct socio-political culture, Kolkata is noted for its revolutionary history, ranging from the Indian struggle for independence to the leftist and trade union movements.

Geography: Kolkata is located in eastern India at 22°332 N, 88°202 E in the Ganges Delta at an elevation ranging between 1.5 to 9 metres. It is spread linearly along the banks of the River Hooghly in a north-south direction. Much of the city was originally a vast wetland, reclaimed over the decades to accommodate the city's burgeoning population. The Sundarbans National Park separates the city from the Bay of Bengal, which is located about 154 km to the south.

Like the most of the Indo-Gangetic plains, the predominant soil type is alluvial. Quaternary sediments consisting of clay, silt, various grades of sand and gravel underlie the city. These sediments are sandwiched between two clay beds, the lower one at depths between 250 and 650 m and the upper one ranging between 10 and 40 m in thickness.

According to the Bureau of Indian Standards, the town falls under seismic zone-III, in a scale of I to V (in order of increasing proneness to earthquakes) while the wind and cyclone zoning is "very high damage risk", according to UNDP report.

Urban Structure: Kolkata city, under the jurisdiction of the Kolkata Municipal Corporation (KMC), has an area of 185 km^2. The Kolkata urban agglomeration, however, has continuously expanded and as of 2006, the urban agglomeration (Kolkata Metropolitan Area) is spread over 1750 km^2 and comprises 157 postal areas.

The urban agglomeration is formally administered by several local governments including 38 local municipalities. The urban agglomeration comprises 72 cities and 527 towns and villages. The suburban areas of Kolkata metropolitan district incorporates parts of the districts North 24 Parganas, South 24 Parganas, Howrah, Hooghly and Nadia.

The east-to-west dimension of the proper city is narrow, stretching from the Hooghly River in the west to roughly the Eastern Metropolitan Bypass in the east, a span of barely 5–6 km. The north-south expansion is roughly divided into North, Central and South Kolkata. North Kolkata locality is the oldest part of the city, with 19th century architecture and narrow alleyways.

The ambience in this area is reminiscent of the old Kolkata. South Kolkata grew mostly after independence and consists of elite localities. The Salt lake City (Bidhan Nagar) area to the northeast of the city is a planned section of Kolkata. Rajarhat, also called New Town, is a planned township being developed on the north-eastern fringes of the city.

Central Kolkata houses the central business district around the B. B. D. Bagh area. The government secretariat, General Post Office, High Court, Lalbazar Police HQs and several other government and private offices are located here.

The Maidan is a large open field in the heart of the city where several sporting events and public meetings are held. Several companies have set up their offices around the area south of Park Street which has become a secondary Central Business District.

Economy: Kolkata is the main business, commercial and financial hub of eastern India and the northeastern states. It is home to the Kolkata Stock Exchange — India's second-largest bourse. It is also a major commercial and military port, and the only city in the region to have an international airport. Once India's leading city and Capital, Kolkata experienced a steady economic decline in the years following India's independence due to the prevalent unstabilised political condition and rise in trade-unionism supported by left-wing parties.

Between the 1960s to the mid 1990s, flight of capital was enormous as many large factories were closed or downsized and businesses relocated. The lack of capital and resources coupled with a worldwide glut in demand in the city's traditional industries (*e.g.* jute) added to the depressed state of the city's economy. The liberalisation of the Indian economy in the 1990s along with the election of a new reformist Chief Minister, Buddhadeb Bhattacharya have resulted in the improvement of the city's fortunes.

Until recently, flexible production had always been the norm in Kolkata, and the informal sector has comprised more than 40% of the labour force. State and federal government employees make up a large percentage of the city's workforce. The city has a large unskilled and semi-skilled labour population, along with other blue-collar and knowledge workers. Kolkata's economic revival was led largely by IT services, with the IT sector growing at 70% yearly — twice that of the national average.

In recent years there has been a surge of investments in the housing infrastructure sector with several new projects coming up in the city. Kolkata is home to many industrial units operated by large Indian corporations with products ranging from electronics to jute. Some notable companies headquartered in Kolkata include ITC Limited, Bata India, Birla Corporation, Coal India Limited, Damodar Valley Corporation, United Bank of India, UCO Bank and Allahabad Bank Vijaya Bank. Recently, various events like adoption of "Look East" policy by the government of India, opening of the Nathu La Pass in Sikkim as a border trade-route with China and immense interest in the South East Asian countries to enter the Indian market and invest have put Kolkata in an advantageous position.

Siliguri

Siliguri is a rapidly developing metropolis in the Indian state of West Bengal. It is strategically located in the Chicken's Neck — a very narrow strip of land linking mainland India to its north eastern states. Besides, it is also the transit point for air, road and rail traffic to the neighbouring countries of Nepal, Bhutan and Bangladesh. The town hosts over 500,000 domestic and 15,000 foreign visitors annually. It is the commercial nerve centre of North Bengal.

Siliguri is situated in Darjeeling district, and though it is the district's largest city, the district headquarters is located at Darjeeling. Siliguri is a unique city as 15 out of 47 wards of Siliguri Municipal Corporation falls in neighbouring Jalpaiguri district. The Indian army, Border Security Force (BSF), Central Reserve Police Force (CRPF), Shashatra Seema Bal (SSB) and the Assam Rifles have bases around the town. The Bagdogra Airport is located within the Indian Air Force (IAF) cantonment area. Siliguri has an Indian Oil Corporation Ltd. (IOC) oil depot near the southern edge of the town. Siliguri is the 2nd largest city of West Bengal after Greater Kolkata.

Geography: Siliguri is situated at the base of the Himalaya mountains in the plains. It is the largest city in the area (North Bengal) and 2nd largest city in west bengal and connects the hill station towns of Gangtok, Kalimpong, Kurseong, Mirik and Darjeeling with the rest of India. The Mahananda River flows past Siliguri. Siliguri has three main seasons summer, winter and monsoon. Summer temperatures rarely exceed 38°C.

It is considerably cooler than the southern and central regions of West Bengal. During this season, tourists from all over India stop in Siliguri en route to the cooler climes of the northern hill stations. Winters are relatively cool and temperatures range from a high of 15°C to a low of about 3°C. Light rain and dense fog are seen during this season. Live Siliguri Weather Conditions During the monsoon season between June and September, the town is lashed by heavy rains often cutting access to the hill stations and Sikkim. The climate is suitable for growing tea and the surrounding region has many tea gardens.

Economy: Siliguri is described as the gateway to the Northeast. The strategic location of the city makes it a base for essential supplies to the region. Siliguri has gradually developed as a profitable centre for a variety of businesses. As a central hub, many national companies and organisations have set up their offices here. Recently a number of movie-multiplexes are being planned to be opened in Siliguri. The Hong Kong market located here is a chief hub for buying low cost Chinese goods and illegal imported goods, nearby Seth Srilal Market is a prominent place to buy daily use goods, and is very popular among people from nearby areas. 3 "T" s - Tea, Timber and Transport are the main businesses of Siliguri. Recently many hotels had mushroomed up & a very good increment had been seen in this sector at past. Siliguri is the headquarters of FOCIN (Fedaration of Chamber of Commerce and Industry of North Bengal).

Bardhaman

Bardhaman is a city of West Bengal state in eastern India. It is the headquarter of Bardhaman District.

Bardhaman has been a district capital since the time of Mughals. Later on it became a district headquarters of British India. Burdwan is an alternative name for the city, which remains in use from the British period.

Geography: Barddhaman is located at 23.25° N 87.85° E. It has an average elevation of 40 metres (131 feet). The city is situated a little less than 100 km north-west of Kolkata on the Grand Trunk Road (NH-2) and Eastern Railway. The chief rivers are the Damodar and Bankanala.

Demographics: As of 2001 India census[GRIndia], Bardhaman had a population of 285,871. Males constitute 52% of the population and females 48%. Bardhaman has an average literacy rate of 77%, higher than the national average of 59.5%; with 55% of the males and 45% of females literate. 9% of the population is under 6 years of age.

Howrah

Howrah (also spelled *Haora*) is an industrial city in West Bengal, India. It is also the name of the Howrah administrative district which includes the city and its surroundings. It is on the west bank of the Hoogli River, and is Kolkata's twin city. It is

West Bengal's second largest city. The two cities are linked by the famous Howrah Bridge (Rabindra Setu), as well as the Vidyasagar Setu (the *second Howrah Bridge*) and the Vivekananda Setu bridges. The city also contains Howrah Station, one of the major train stations serving Kolkata as well as Howrah.

Geography: Howrah is located at 22.59° N 88.31° E. It has an average elevation of 12 metres (39 feet).

Demographics: As of 2001 India census[GRIndia], Howrah had a population of 1,008,704. Males constitute 54% of the population and females 46%. Howrah has an average literacy rate of 77%, higher than the national average of 59.5%: male literacy is 81%, and female literacy is 73%. In Howrah, 9% of the population is under 6 years of age.

Durgapur

Durgapur is an industrial township in the state of West Bengal, India, located about 160 km from Kolkata. It was a dream child of the great visionary Dr. Bidhan Chandra Roy, the second chief minister of the state. The well laid out industrial township was designed by Joseph Allen Stein and Benjamin Polk. It is home to the largest industrial unit in the state, Durgapur Steel Plant, one of the integrated steel plants of Steel Authority of India Limited. Alloy Steel Plant of SAIL is also located here. There are a number of power plants, chemical and engineering industries. Some metallurgical units have come up in recent years. Durgapur is the third largest city of West Bengal after Kolkata and Asansol.

Geography: Durgapur is located at 23.48° N 87.32° E. It has an average elevation of 65 metres (213 feet).

Durgapur is situated on the bank of river Damodar, just before it enters the alluvial plains of Bengal. The topography is undulating. The coal-bearing area of the Ranigunj coalfields lies just beyond Durgapur, although some parts intrude in to the area. The area was deeply forested till recent times, and some forests are still there, standing witness to its wild past.

Two mighty rivers border it on the north and south. The Ajay River flows past unhindered in the north but the Damodar River on the south has two obstacles in its path – an earlier anicut at Rondia and a more recent barrage at Durgapur. Two rivulets, Singaran and Tamla, flow through the area and join the Damodar. Two other rivulets in the area, Kunur and Tumuni, join the Ajay.

Durgapur subdivision is surrounded by Asansol subdivision on the west, Bardhaman sadar subdivision on the east, Bankura district across the Damodar in the south, and Birbhum district across the Ajay to the north.

The Grand Trunk Road (NH2) virtually bifurcates the area. It has now been widened as part of the Golden Quadrilateral project. Another wide road takes off from Darjeeling Morh near Panagarh for North Bengal. It also links Santiniketan to the Grand Trunk Road. The Durgapur Expressway, linking Dankuni with Memari on Grand Trunk Road, now allows fast communication between Kolkata and Durgapur. A road over the Durgapur barrage links Durgapur with Bankura and beyond in South Bengal.

The Kolkata-Delhi railway track passes through Durgapur. Andal has a link with Sainthia on the Sahibgunj loop line. There are airstrips at Panagarh and Durgapur, the former with the Indian Air Force and latter with SAIL.

Haldia

Haldia is a city and a municipality in Purba Medinipur in the Indian state of West Bengal. It is a major seaport located approximately 50 kilometers southwest of Kolkata near the mouth of the Hooghly River, one of the distributaries of the Ganges.

Haldia is being developed as a major trade port for Kolkata, intended mainly for bulk cargoes. The population (1991) is 100,109.

Haldia is now become a centre for development of West Bengal. The industrial city has several factories like Indian Oil Corporation Limited (IOCL), Exide, Shaw Wallace, Tata Chemicals, Petrochemical complex (Haldia Petrochemical) and Hindustan

Lever, in addition to various light industries.

The port has attracted factories of foreign companies, like Mitsubishi Chemical Company (MCC).

A large number of companies are also being set up now, primarily being ancillary industries to the Haldia Petrochemicals.

The Haldia Petrochemicals is the second largest project of such kind in India. Mr. S. K. Bhowmik is the Managing Director and Mr. Ujjal De is the V. P & Head-Marketing.

Haldia as a city is a modern one and it is growing very fast. The Haldia Township is bordered by the Haldi River an offshoot of the Ganges River.

The riverside in Haldia is a favourite destination for residents and one can see people strolling down the riverside during the evenings. A catamaran service direct from Kolkata to Haldia was in service. It was later withdrawn due to its high price and decreasing number of passengers.

Haldia is also a base of Indian Coast Guard. There is a hover-port to house two of the six hovercrafts belonging to the Indian Coast Guard.

Geography: Haldia is located at 22.03° N 88.06° E. It has an average elevation of 8 metres (26 feet).

Demographics: As of 2001 India census[GRIndia], Haldia had a population of 170,695. Males constitute 53% of the population and females 47%. Haldia has an average literacy rate of 72%, higher than the national average of 59.5%: male literacy is 79%, and female literacy is 98%. In Haldia, 13% of the population is under 6 years of age.

Kharagpur

Kharagpur (KGP) pronunciation is a town in India. It is located in the Midnapore West district of the state of West Bengal. Features that distinguish it from the multitude of other small towns spanning India are its railway platform, purportedly the longest railway platform (1.072 km or 3,517 feet) in the world.

It is the most important station of the South Eastern Railway, originating from Howrah Station, the tracks trifurcate here for Tatanagar (going west towards Nagpur, SE Railway was formerly known as *BNR* or *Bengal Nagpur Railway*), Midnapore (going north) and Balasore (heading southwards along the coast of the Bay of Bengal).

Kharagpur was chosen as the location of the first campus of the prestigious Indian Institutes of Technology (IITs). The IITs are the premier technical education institutes in India and are internationally recognised for their academic and technical excellence. Unlike other IITs, IIT Kharagpur has been long known for its ability to offer unusual courses not offered in other IITs. It also has a reputation for student bonding, unique hostel life and extensive extracurricular activities. The campus is located in Hijli.

Kharagpur also has one of the biggest Railway workshops in India which includes all the workshops for A-Z of Railways.

Location: Kharagpur lies on the latitude of 22 02' 30" & longitude 87 11' 0", covering an area of about 3000 km^2 located in the south-west part of Midnapore. This sub-division town is formed with Dalma Pahar and alluvial tract of Midnapore. It is intersected by numerous waterways, the important rivers being Subarnarekha, Keleghai and Kangsabati River.

Geography: Kharagpur is located at 22.33° N 87.33° E. It has an average elevation of 29 metres (95 feet).

Baharampur

Baharampur (also spelled Berhampore or Berhampur) is a city in the West Bengal state of India. Baharampur is the administrative headquarters of the Murshidabad district.

Geography: Baharampur is located at 24.1° N 88.25° E. It has an average elevation of 18 metres (59 feet).

The city is located approximately 185 km north of Kolkata at 24°42 N, 88°92 E and is situated on the east side of the Bhagirathi River, a major tributary of the Ganges. The city's industries include silk weaving, ivory carving, rice and oil-seed milling, and precious-metal working,Bell Metal from Khagra called "Khagrai Kansha" is famous and special type of fried sweets called "Chanabora" is also very popular. It is also a rail and road hub of the West Bengal state and is an important agricultural centre.

Demographics: As of 2001 India census[GRIndia], Baharampur had a population of 160,168. Males constitute 51% of the population and females 49%. Baharampur has an average literacy rate of 79%, higher than the national average of 59.5%; with 53% of the males and 47% of females literate. 9% of the population is under 6 years of age.

Trivia-Baharampur is famous for the sweetmeat 'Chhana-bora' and the savoury 'Khaja'.

Purulia

Purulia is a town located in West Bengal state, India. It is the location of the district headquarters of Purulia district. Purulia is located on the north of the Kasai river and is a major road and railway junction. Purulia municipality was constituted in 1876.

Geography: Puruliya is located at 23.33° N 86.37° E. It has an average elevation of 228 metres (748 feet).

Demographics: As of 2001 India census[GRIndia], Puruliya had a population of 113,766. Males constitute 52% of the population and females 48%,. Puruliya has an average literacy rate of 68%, higher than the national average of 59.5%: male literacy is 76%, and female literacy is 60%, one of the highest literacy rate in India. In Puruliya, 12% of the population is under 6 years of age.

Jhalda

Jhalda is a city and a municipality in Purulia District in the Indian state of West Bengal.

Demographics: As of 2001 India census[GRIndia], Jhalda had a population of 17,870. Males constitute 52% of the population and females 48%. Jhalda has an average literacy rate of 64%, higher than the national average of 59.5%: male literacy is 73%, and female literacy is 53%. In Jhalda, 14% of the population is under 6 years of age.

DARJEELING HIMALAYAN HILL REGION

Darjeeling Himalayan hill region is situated on the North-Western side of the state of West Bengal in India. This region belongs to the Eastern Himalaya range. The whole of the Darjeeling district except the Siliguri division constitutes the region. It starts abruptly up from the Terai region.

The region slopes up from a south to north direction. The river Teesta divides the region in two parts— The region to the east of Teesta and The region to the west of Teesta.

Hills to the West of Teesta

The highest region of the Darjeeling Himalaya, two distinct ranges are visible here—the Singalila range and the Darjeeling-karsiang range.

Singalila Range

The Singalila range is on the western limit of the region and separates Nepal from West Bengal. Singalila National Park is situated here. The 4 highest peaks are :

1. Falut (3,595 m)
2. Sandakfu (3,630 m) — The highest point of West Bengal.
3. Tonglu (3,036 m)
4. Sabargram (3,543 m)

Darjeeling-karsiang Range

Two notable peaks are Tiger Hill and Sinchal.

Hills to the East of Teesta

The Chola range is situated on the Sikkim and Bhutan

border. The highest peak is Rishila. The city of Kalimpong is situated in this region, while the relatively low height Buxa-Jayanti range, a part of the Sivalik, is also located here.

Rivers

Some notable rivers of this region are Teesta, Jaldhaka, balason, Mechi, Lis, Ghis, Raidak, etc.

Terai Region

The Tarai ("moist land") is a belt of marshy grasslands, savannas, and forests at the base of the Himalaya range in India, Nepal, and Bhutan, from the Yamuna River in the west to the Brahmaputra River in the east. Above the Terai belt lies the Bhabhar, a forested belt of rock, gravel, and soil eroded from the Himalayas, where the water table lies from 5 to 37 meters deep. The Terai zone lies below the Bhabhar, and is composed of alternate layers of clay and sand, with a high water table that creates many springs and wetlands. The Terai zone is inundated yearly by the monsoon-swollen rivers of the Himalaya. Below the Terai lies the great alluvial plain of the Yamuna, Ganges, Brahmaputra, and their tributaries.

Terai-Duar Savanna and Grasslands

The Terai-Duar savanna and grasslands is an ecoregion that stretches across the middle of the Terai belt, from Uttarakhand state through southern Nepal to northern West Bengal. The Terai-Duar savanna and wetlands are a mosaic of tall grasslands, savannas and evergreen and deciduous forests. The grasslands are among the tallest in the world, and are maintained by silt deposited by the yearly monsoon floods. Important grasses include Kans grass *(Saccharum spontaneum)* and Baruwa grass *(Saccharum benghalensis)*. The ecoregion is home to the endangered Indian Rhinoceros *(Rhinoceros unicornis)*, as well as elephants, tigers, bears, leopards and other wild animals. Much of the ecoregion has been converted to farmland, although Royal Chitwan National Park and Royal Bardia National Park preserve significant sections of habitat, and are home to some of the greatest concentrations of rhinoceros and tiger remaining in South Asia.

GEOGRAPHY AND CLIMATE

Many areas remain flooded during the heavy rains brought by a monsoon.

West Bengal is on the eastern bottleneck of India, stretching from the Himalayas in the north to the Bay of Bengal in the south. The state has a total area of 88,752 square kilometres (34,267 sq mi). The Darjeeling Himalayan hill region in the northern extreme of the state is a part of the eastern Himalayas mountain range. In this region is Sandakfu, which, at 3,636 m (11,929 ft), is the highest peak in the state. The narrow Terai region separates the hills from the North Bengal plains, which in turn transitions into the Ganges delta towards the south. The Rarh region intervenes between the Ganges delta in the east and the western plateau and high lands. A small coastal region is in the extreme south, while the Sundarbans mangrove forests form a geographical landmark at the Ganges delta.

The main river in West Bengal is the Ganges, which divides into two branches. One branch enters Bangladesh as the *Padma*, or *Pôdda*, while the other flows through West Bengal as the Bhagirathi River and Hooghly River. The Farakka barrage over the Ganges feeds the Hooghly branch of the river by a feeder canal, and its water flow management has been a source of lingering dispute between India and Bangladesh. The Teesta, Torsa, Jaldhaka, and Mahananda rivers are in the northern hilly region.

The western plateau region has rivers such as the Damodar, Ajay, and Kangsabati. The Ganges delta and the Sundarbans area have numerous rivers and creeks. Pollution of the Ganges from indiscriminate waste dumped into the river is a major problem. Damodar, another tributary of the Ganges and once known as the "Sorrow of Bengal" (due to its frequent floods), has several dams under the Damodar Valley Project. At least nine districts in the state suffer from arsenic contamination of groundwater, and as of 2017, an estimated 1.04 crore people were afflicted by arsenic poisioning

West Bengal's climate varies from tropical savanna in the southern portions to humid subtropical in the north. The main seasons are summer, the rainy season, a short autumn, and winter. While the summer in the delta region is noted for excessive humidity, the western highlands experience a dry summer like northern India, with the highest daytime temperature ranging from 38 °C (100 °F) to 45 °C (113 °F).

At night, a cool southerly breeze carries moisture from the Bay of Bengal. In early summer, brief squalls and thunderstorms known as *Kalbaisakhi*, or Nor'westers, often occur. West Bengal receives the Bay of Bengal branch of the Indian Ocean monsoon that moves in a southeast to northwest direction. Monsoons bring rain to the whole state from June to September. Heavy rainfall of above 250 centimetres (98 in) is observed in the Darjeeling, Jalpaiguri, and Cooch Behar district. During the arrival of the monsoons, low pressure in the Bay of Bengal region often leads to the formation of storms in the coastal areas. Winter (December–January) is mild over the plains with average minimum temperatures of 15 °C (59 °F). A cold and dry northern wind blows in the winter, substantially lowering the humidity level. The Darjeeling Himalayan Hill region experiences a harsh winter, with occasional snowfall.

FLORA AND FAUNA

A Bengal tiger

Sal trees in the Arabari forest in West Midnapur

As per the India State of Forest Report 2017, recorded forest area in the state is 16,847 km (6,505 sq mi), while in 2013, forest area was 16,805 km (6,488 sq mi), which was 18.93% of the state's geographical area, compared to the then national average of 21.23%.Reserves and protected and unclassed forests constitute 59.4%, 31.8%, and 8.9%, respectively, of forested areas, as of 2009. Part of the world's largest mangrove forest, the Sundarbans is located in southern West Bengal.

From a phytogeographic viewpoint, the southern part of West Bengal can be divided into two regions: the Gangetic plain and the littoral mangrove forests of the Sundarbans. The alluvial soil of the Gangetic plain, combined with favourable rainfall, makes this region especially fertile. Much of the vegetation of the western part of the state has similar species composition with the plants of the Chota Nagpur plateau in the adjoining state of Jharkhand. The predominant commercial tree species is *Shorea robusta*, commonly known as the sal tree. The coastal region of Purba Medinipurexhibits coastal vegetation; the predominant tree is the *Casuarina*. A notable tree from the Sundarbans is the ubiquitous *sundari* (*Heritiera fomes*), from which the forest gets its name.

The distribution of vegetation in northern West Bengal is dictated by elevation and precipitation. For example, the foothills of the Himalayas, the *Dooars*, are densely wooded with sal and other tropical evergreen trees.Above an elevation of 1,000 metres (3,300 ft), the forest becomes predominantly subtropical. In Darjeeling, which is above 1,500 metres (4,900 ft), temperate forest trees such as oaks, conifers, and rhododendrons predominate.

3.26% of the geographical area of West Bengal is protected land, comprising fifteen wildlife sanctuaries and five national parks – Sundarbans National Park, Buxa Tiger Reserve, Gorumara National Park, Neora Valley National Park, and Singalila National Park. Extant wildlife include Indian rhinoceros, Indian elephant, deer, leopard, gaur, tiger, and crocodiles, as well as many bird species. Migratory birds come to the state during the winter. The high-altitude forests of Singalila National Park shelter barking deer, red panda, chinkara, takin, serow, pangolin, minivet, and kalij pheasants. The Sundarbans are noted for a reserve project devoted to conserving the endangered Bengal tigeralthough the forest hosts many other endangered species such as the Gangetic dolphin, river terrapin, and estuarine crocodile. The mangrove forest also acts as a natural fish nursery, supporting coastal fishes along the Bay of Bengal. Recognising its special conservation value, the Sundarbans area has been declared a Biosphere Reserve.

NORTH BENGAL PLAINS

North Bengal plains starts from the south of Terai region and continues up to the left bank of the Ganges. The southern parts of the district Jalpaiguri, North Dinajpur baring some extreme northern regions, South Dinajpur, Malda and Cooch Behar districts constitute this geographical region.

RARH REGION

Rarh region of West Bengal is the region that intervenes between the Western plateau and high lands and the Ganges Delta. Parts of the districts Murshidabad, Birbhum, Bankura, Bardhaman and Medinipur constitutes this region. The region is about 50 to 100 m above the sea level.

History of the Name

The west coast of Bhagirathi was called Radha/ Rarha/ Ladha/ Lara. The western side of Rarh is sometimes separated into Vajjabhumi (Bajrabhumi) which is the eastern fringe of the Chhotanagpur plateau, to demarcate from the eastern part of the Rarh called Sumhabhumi or Subbabhumi. The oldest Jain book of codes Acharanga Sutra and Buddhist Jataka mentions about these regions.

According to Acharanga Sutra Mahavira travelled in the pathless country of 'Ladha' in Vajjabhumi and Subbhabhumi at a time (5th Century BC) when the country was lawless and the people were harsh at Mahavir. Alexander the great was supposed to have been discouraged to come to eastern India due to the power of the "Gangaridai" or "Ganga Rarh's who were probably the people of Rarh According to Bengali Historian Dr. Atul Sur. Pleeny and Ptolemy also mention about "Ganga Rarh"s. Gangaridai has been spelled differently by different Greek/Roman accounts: Gangaridae, Gandaridai, Gangaritai, Gangaridum.

However the stem of the term Gangaridai is Ganga which has been interpreted by different historians as: Ganga-Hrd (Land with Ganges in its heart), Ganga-Rashtra (State of the

Ganges), Gandaridai (Land of the Gonds). The Bhuvaneshvara inscription of Bhavadeva Bhatta records that "Radha was a waterless, dry and woody region".

Rakhaldas Bandyopadhyay, the famous Bengali historian says: "During Chandragupta Maurya's rule Gangaridai was independent like the Andhra kingdom and Gangaridai was joined with kalinga." It is interesting that the description of the Armed forces of Gangaridae and Calingae during the reign of Chandragupta Maurya as given by Megasthenes are identical (both possessed army of 60,000 foot-soldiers, 1,000 horsemen and 700 elephants). A statement in Dig-vijaya-prakasha locates to Radha the north of River Damodar and to the south of Gauda. Tabaqat-i-Nasiri also suggests that the Radha region lay to the west of the Ganges. Dipavangsha and Mahavangsha state that Sri Lanka was colonised by Vijaya Simha who hailed from Simhapura in 'Lala' (Rarh).

Geology

This region is believed to be created from the soil from the Deccan plateau. Red coloured laterite soil is predominant. The silts of the soil are coarse. The soil is not mush suitable for agriculture as the alkalinity is high and organic material is comparatively less.

Rivers

The most notable rivers are Damodar, Ajay, Mayurakshi, Dwarakeshwar, Shilai and Kasai. All the river originates from Chhotanagpur Plateau and flows towards east or south-east finally to meet River Hooghly. The river Subarnarekha flows through some parts of the region and ends at the Bay of Bengal. In the past, some of the rivers were notorious for causing flood. With the construction of several dams, the floods have been somewhat controlled.

COASTAL PLAIN

In geography, a coastal plain is an area of flat, low-lying land adjacent to a seacoast and separated from the interior by other features. One of the world's longest coastal plains is located in western South America. The southeastern coastal plain of North America is notable for its species diversity. The Gulf Coastal Plain of North America extends northwards from the Gulf of Mexico along the Lower Mississippi River to the Ohio River, which is a distance of about 500 miles (about 800 km). During the Cretaceous age, the central area of the United States was covered by a shallow sea, which disappeared as the land rose. Large fossilized aquatic birds called *Hesperornis* and *Ichthyornis*, found in western Kansas, indicate that the shallow sea was rife with fish. The coastal plain lying alongside the lower Mississippi River may be associated with the shallow sea which had existed 100 million years ago.

SUNDARBANS

The Sundarbans delta is the largest mangrove forest in the world. It lies at the mouth of the Ganges and is spread across areas of Bangladesh and West Bengal, India, forming the seaward fringe of the delta. Interestingly, the Bangladesh and Indian portion of the jungle are listed in the UNESCO world heritage list separately as the Sundarbans and Sundarbans National Park respectively, though they are simply parts of the same forest.

The Sundarbans is intersected by a complex network of tidal waterways, mudflats and small islands of salt-tolerant mangrove forests, and presents an excellent example of ongoing ecological processes. The area is known for its wide range of fauna. The most famous among these are the man-eating Royal Bengal Tigers, but numerous species of birds, spotted deer, crocodiles and snakes also inhabit it. It is estimated that there are now 400 Bengal tigers and about 30,000 spotted deer in the area.

Most of the plot of prize-winning anthropologist Amitav Ghosh's 2004 novel, *The Hungry Tide*, is set in the Sundarbans.

During each monsoon season almost all the Bengali delta is submerged, much of it for half a year. The sediment of the lower delta plain is primarily advected inland by monsoonal coastal setup and cyclonic events. One of the greatest challenges people living on the Ganges Delta may face in coming years is the threat of rising sea levels caused mostly by subsidence in the region and partly by climate change. Residents have to be careful building on the river delta, as severe flooding sometimes occurs. A 1990 study noted "There is no evidence that environmental degradation in the Himalayas or a 'greenhouse'-induced rise in sea level have aggravated floods in Bangladesh." Upstream dams can reduce fresh water supply.

In many of the Indian mangrove wetlands, freshwater reaching the mangroves was considerably reduced from the late 19th century due to diversion of freshwater in the upstream area. Also, the Bengal Basin is slowly tilting towards the east due to neo-tectonic movement, forcing greater freshwater input to the Bangladesh Sunderbans. As a result, the salinity of the Bangladesh Sunderbans is much lower than that of the Indian Sunderbans.

Etymology

Sundarbans literally means "beautiful forest" in Bengali language. The name Sundarbans may also have been derived from the Sundari trees that are found in Sundarbans in large numbers.

History

In 1911 it was described as a tract of waste country which had never been surveyed, nor had the census been extended to it. It then stretched for about 165 miles from the mouth of the Hugli to the mouth of the Meghna, and was bordered inland by the three settled districts of the Twenty-four Parganas, Khulna and Backergunje. The total area (including water) was estimated at 6526 square miles. It was a water-logged jungle, in which tigers and other wild beasts abounded. Attempts at reclamation had not been very successful.

The characteristic tree was the *sundri* (*Heritiera littoralis*), from which the name of the tract had probably been derived.

It yields a hard wood, sued for building, and for making boats, furniture, etc. The Sundarbans were everywhere intersected by river channels and creeks, some of which afforded water communication between Kolkata and the Brahmaputra valley, both for steamers and for native boats.

Ecosystem

The mangrove-dominated Ganges delta – the Sundarbans - is a complex ecosystem comprising one of the three largest single tract of mangrove forests of the world. Shared between two neighbouring countries, Bangladesh and India, the larger part (62%) is situated in the southwest corner of Bangladesh. To the south the forest meets the Bay of Bengal; to the east it is bordered by the Baleswar River and to the north there is a sharp interface with intensively cultivated land. The natural drainage in the upstream areas, other than the main river channels, is everywhere impeded by extensive embankments and polders.

The total land area is 4,143 km² (including exposed sandbars: 42 km²) and the remaining water area of 1,874 km² encompasses rivers, small streams and canals. Rivers in the Sundarbans are meeting places of salt water and freshwater. Thus, it is a region of transition between the freshwater of the rivers originating from the Ganges and the saline water of the Bay of Bengal (Wahid *et al.*. 2002).

In terms of biodiversity, the Sundarbans contrasts the other large mangrove forests for its extraordinarily diverse wildlife and designated as a UNESCO's World Network of International Biosphere Reserves since 2001.

The forest also has immense protective and productive functions. Constituting 51% of the total reserved forest estate of Bangladesh it contributes about 41% of total forest revenue and accounts for about 45% of all timber and fuel wood output of the country (FAO 1995). A number of industries (*e.g.* newsprint mill, match factory, hardboard, boat building, furniture making) are based on the raw material obtained from the Sundarbans ecosystem. Various non-timber forest products and plantations help generate considerable employment and income generation opportunities for at least half a million poor coastal population. Besides production functions of the forest, it provides natural protection to life and properties of the coastal population in cyclone prone Bangladesh.

The Sundarbans has a population of over 4 million but much of it is mostly free of permanent human habitation and retained a forest closure of about 70% according to the Overseas Development Administration (ODA) of the United Kingdom in 1985, forest inventories reveal a decline in standing volume of the two main commercial mangrove species—sundri (*Heritiera fomes*) and gewa (*Excoecaria agallocha*)—by 40% and 45% respectively between 1959 and 1983 (Forestal 1960 and ODA 1985). Also, despite a total ban on all killing or capture of wildlife other than fish and some invertebrates, there appears to be a pattern of depleted biodiversity or loss of species (notably at least six mammals and one important reptile this century), and that the "ecological quality of the original mangrove forest is declining" (IUCN 1994).

Tigers

The Sundarbans are home to approximately 400 Bengal Tigers as of 2004. These tigers are well-known for the substantial number of people they kill; estimates range from 100-250 people per year. They are the only man-eating tigers left in the world, though they are not the only tigers who live in close proximity to humans. In Bandhavgarh, villages encircle the tiger reserves, and yet attacks on people are rare.

The locals and government officials take certain precautions to prevent attacks, although few of them work. Local fishermen will say prayers and perform rituals to the forest god, Bonbibi, before setting out on expeditions. Fishermen and bushmen make facial masks to wear on the back of their heads, due to the fact that tigers always attack from behind. This worked for a short time, but the tigers quickly realized it was a hoax, and the attacks continued. Government officials wear stiff pads that rise up the back of the neck, similar to the pads of an American football player. This is to prevent the tigers from biting into the spine, which is their favoured attack method.

There are several speculated causes as to why these tigers maul humans:

- Since the Sundarbans is located in a coastal area, the water is relatively salty. In all other habitats, tigers drink fresh water. It is rumoured that the saltiness of the tiger's water in this area has put them in a state of constant discomfort, leading them to be extremely aggressive. Freshwater lakes have been artificially made but to no avail.
- The high tides in the area destroy the tiger's scents which serve as territorial markers. Thus, the only way for a tiger to defend its territory is to physically dominate everything that enters.
- Another possibility is that these tigers have grown used to human flesh due to the weather. Floods in this part of India kill thousands, and the bodies drift out in to the swampy waters, where tigers scavenge on them.
- Another possibility is that the tigers find hunting animals difficult due to the continuous high & low tides making the area marsh-like and slippery. Humans travel through the Sunderbans on boats gathering honey and fishing, making an easy or accessible prey. It is also believed that when a person stops to work, the tiger mistakes them for an animal, and has, over time, acquired a 'taste' for the human flesh.

6

Economy

ECONOMY

Most tribes are concentrated in heavily forested areas that combine inaccessibility with limited political or economic significance. Historically, the economy of most tribes was subsistence agriculture or hunting and gathering. Tribal members traded with outsiders for the few necessities they lacked, such as salt and iron. A few local Hindu craftsmen might provide such items as cooking utensils.

In the early 20th century, however, large areas fell into the hands of non-tribals, on account of improved transportation and communications. Around 1900, many regions were opened by the government to settlement through a scheme by which inward migrants received ownership of land free in return for cultivating it. For tribal people, however, land was often viewed as a common resource, free to whoever needed it.

By the time tribals accepted the necessity of obtaining formal land titles, they had lost the opportunity to lay claim to lands that might rightfully have been considered theirs. The colonial and post-independence regimes belatedly realized the necessity of protecting tribals from the predations of outsiders and prohibited the sale of tribal lands. Although an important loophole in the form of land leases was left open, tribes made some gains in the mid-twentieth century, and some land was returned to tribal peoples despite obstruction by local police and land officials.

In the 1970s, tribal peoples came again under intense land pressure, especially in central India. Migration into tribal lands increased dramatically, as tribal people lost title to their lands in many ways – lease, forfeiture from debts, or bribery of land registry officials. Other non-tribals simply squatted, or even lobbied governments to classify them as tribal to allow them to compete with the formerly established tribes.

The Grand Hotel in Kolkata. Tourism, especially from Bangladesh, is an important part of West Bengal's economy.

In any case, many tribal members became landless labourers in the 1960s and 1970s, and regions that a few years earlier had been the exclusive domain of tribes had an increasingly mixed population of tribals and non-tribals. Government efforts to evict nontribal members from illegal occupation have proceeded slowly; when evictions occur at all, those ejected are usually members of poor, lower castes.

Improved communications, roads with motorized traffic, and more frequent government intervention figured in the increased contact that tribal peoples had with outsiders. Commercial highways and cash crops frequently drew non-tribal people into remote areas. By the 1960s and 1970s, the resident nontribal shopkeeper was a permanent feature of many tribal villages.

Since shopkeepers often sell goods on credit (demanding high interest), many tribal members have been drawn deeply into debt or mortgaged their land. Merchants also encourage tribals to grow cash crops (such as cotton or castor-oil plants), which increases tribal dependence on the market for basic necessities. Indebtedness is so extensive that although such transactions are illegal, traders sometimes 'sell' their debtors to other merchants, much like indentured peons.

The final blow for some tribes has come when nontribals, through political jockeying, have managed to gain legal tribal status, that is, to be listed as a Scheduled Tribe.

Tribes in the Himalayan foothills have not been as hard-pressed by the intrusions of non-tribals. Historically, their political status was always distinct from the rest of India. Until the British colonial period, there was little effective control by any of the empires centered in peninsular India; the region was populated by autonomous feuding tribes.

The British, in efforts to protect the sensitive northeast frontier, followed a policy dubbed the "Inner Line"; nontribal people were allowed into the areas only with special permission. Postindependence governments have continued the policy, protecting the Himalayan tribes as part of the strategy to secure the border with China.

Government policies on forest reserves have affected tribal peoples profoundly. Government efforts to reserve forests have precipitated armed (if futile) resistance on the part of the tribal peoples involved. Intensive exploitation of forests has often meant allowing outsiders to cut large areas of trees (while the original tribal inhabitants were restricted from cutting), and ultimately replacing mixed forests capable of sustaining tribal life with single-product plantations. Nontribals have frequently bribed local officials to secure effective use of reserved forest lands.

The northern tribes have thus been sheltered from the kind of exploitation that those elsewhere in South Asia have suffered. In Arunachal Pradesh (formerly part of the North-East Frontier Agency), for example, tribal members control commerce and most lower-level administrative posts. Government construction projects in the region have provided tribes with a significant source of cash.

Some tribes have made rapid progress through the education system (the role of early missionaries was significant in this regard). Instruction was begun in Assamese but was eventually changed to Hindi; by the early 1980s, English was taught at most levels. Northeastern tribal people have thus enjoyed a certain measure of social mobility.

As of 2015, West Bengal has the sixth-highest GSDP in India. GSDP at current prices (base 2004–2005) has increased from Rs 2,08,656 crores in 2004–05 to Rs 8,00,868 crores in 2014–2015,reaching Rs 10,21,000 crores in 2017-18. GSDP percent growth at current prices has varied from a low of 10.3% in 2010–2011 to a high of 17.11% in 2013–2014. The growth rate was 13.35% in 2014–2015. The state's per capita income has lagged the all India average for over two decades. As of 2014–2015, per capita NSDP at current prices was Rs 78,903. Per capita NSDP growth rate at current prices has varied from 9.4% in 2010–2011 to a high of 16.15% in 2013–2014. The growth rate was 12.62% in 2014–2015.

In 2015–2016, percentage share of Gross Value Added (GVA) at factor cost by Economic Activity at constant price (base year 2011–2012) was Agriculture-Forestry and Fishery – 4.84%, Industry 18.51% and Services 66.65%. It has been observed that there has been a slow but steady decline in the percentage share of industry and agriculture over the years. Agriculture is the leading economic sector in West Bengal. Rice is the state's principal food crop. Rice, potato, jute, sugarcane, and wheat are the top five crops of the state. Tea is produced commercially in northern districts; the region is well known for Darjeeling and other high quality teas. State industries are localised in the Kolkata region, the mineral-rich western highlands, and the Haldia port region. The Durgapur–Asansol colliery belt is home to a number of steel plants. Important manufacturing industries are engineering products, electronics, electrical equipment, cables, steel, leather, textiles, jewellery, frigates, automobiles, railway coaches, and wagons. The Durgapur centre has established a number of industries in the areas of tea, sugar, chemicals, and fertilisers. Natural resources like tea and jute in and nearby parts has made West Bengal a major centre for the jute and tea industries.

Freshly sown saplings of rice in a paddy; in the background are stacks of jute sticks.

Years after independence, West Bengal is dependent on the central government for help in meeting its demands for food; food production remained stagnant, and the Indian green revolution bypassed the state. However, there has been a significant increase in food production since the 1980s, and the state now has a surplus of grains. The state's share of total industrial output in India was 9.8% in 1980–1981, declining to 5% by 1997–1998. In contrast, the service sector has grown at a rate higher than the national rate. The state's total financial debt stood at 1,918,350 million (US$27 billion) as of 2011.

In the period 2004–2010, the average gross state domestic product (GSDP) growth rate was 13.9% (calculated in Indian rupee terms) lower than 15.5%, the average for all states of the country.

The economy of West Bengal has witnessed many twists and turns. The agricultural sector in particular rose to 8.33% in 2010–11 before tumbling down to "4.01 % in 2012–13. Many major industries such as the Uttarpara Hindustan Motors car manufacturing unit, the jute industry, and the Haldia Petrochemicals unit experienced shutdowns in 2014. In the same year, plans for a 30,000 crore Jindal Steel project was mothballed. The tea industry of West Bengal has also witnessed shutdowns due to financial and political reasons. The tourism industry of West Bengal took a hit in 2017 due to the Gorkhaland agitation.

However, over the years due to effective changes in the stance towards industrialisation, ease of doing business has improved in West Bengal. Steps are being taken to remedy this situation by promoting West Bengal as an investment destination. A leather complex has been built in Kolkata, smart cities are being planned closed to Kolkata and major roadway projects are in the offing to revive the economy. West Bengal has been able to attract 2% of the foreign direct investment in the last decade.

AGRICULTURE

Agriculture is the leading occupation in West Bengal. Rice is the state's principal food crop. Other food crops are maize, pulses, oil seeds, wheat, barley, potatoes and vegetables. Jute is the main cash crop of the region. Tea is also produced commercially;

the region is well known for Darjeeling and other high quality teas. Tobacco and sugarcane are also grown.

However, the service sector is the largest contributor to the gross domestic product of the state, contributing 51% of the state domestic product compared to 27% from agriculture and 22% from industry. State industries are localized in the Kolkata region and the mineral-rich western highlands. Durgapur–Asansol colliery belt is home to a number of major steel plants. Manufacturing industries playing an important economic role are engineering products, electronics, electrical equipment, cables, steel, leather, textiles, jewellery, frigates, automobiles, railway coaches, and wagons.

A significant part of the state is economically backward, namely, large parts of six northern districts of Cooch Behar, Darjeeling, Jalpaiguri, Malda, North Dinajpur and South Dinajpur; three western districts of Purulia, Bankura, Birbhum; and the Sundarbans area.

Years after independence, West Bengal was still dependent on the central government for meeting its demands for food; food production remained stagnant and the green revolution bypassed the state. However, there has been a significant spurt in food production since the 1980s, and the state now has a surplus of grains. The state's share of total industrial output in India was 9.8% in 1980–81, declining to 5% by 1997–98. However, the service sector has grown at a rate higher than the national rate.

West Bengal has the third largest economy (2003–2004) in India, with a net state domestic product of US$ 21.5 billion. During 2001–2002, the state's average SDP was more than 7.8% — outperforming the National GDP Growth. The state has promoted foreign direct investment, which has mostly come in the software and electronics fields; Kolkata is becoming a major hub for the Information technology (IT) industry. Owing to the boom in Kolkata's and the overall state's economy, West Bengal is now the third fastest growing economy in the country. However, the rapid industrialisation process has given rise to debate over land acquisition for industry in this agrarian state. NASSCOM–Gartner ranks West Bengal power infrastructure the best in the country.

TRANSPORT

The total length of surface road in West Bengal is over 92,023 km (57,180 mi); national highways comprise 2,377 km (1,477 mi) and state highways 2,393 km (1,487 mi). Average speed on state highways varies between 40–50 km/h (25–31 mi/h); in villages and towns, speeds are as low as 20-25 km/h (12–16 mi/h) due to the proliferation of speed bumps. Total railway length is 3,825 km (2,377 mi); Kolkata is the headquarters of two divisions of the Indian Railways—Eastern Railway and South Eastern Railway. The Northeast Frontier Railway plies in the northern parts of the state. The Kolkata metro is the country's first underground railway, and the Darjeeling Himalayan Railway (NFR) is a UNESCO World Heritage Site.

The state's only international airport is Netaji Subhash Chandra Bose International Airport at Dum Dum, Kolkata. Bagdogra airport near Siliguri is another significant airport in the state. Kolkata is a major river-port in eastern India. The Kolkata Port Trust manages both the Kolkata docks and the Haldia docks. There is passenger service to Port Blair on the Andaman and Nicobar Islands and cargo ship service to ports in India and abroad, operated by the Shipping Corporation of India. Ferry is a principal mode of transport in the southern part of the state, especially in the Sundarbans area. Kolkata is the only city in India to have trams as a mode of transport and these are operated by the Kolkata Tramways Company.

Several government-owned organisations operate bus services in the state, including the Kolkata State Transport Corporation, the North Bengal State Transport Corporation, the South Bengal State Transport Corporation, and the West Bengal Surface Transport Corporation. There are also private bus companies. The railway system is a nationalised service without any private investment. Hired forms of mechanised transport include metered taxis and auto rickshaws which often ply specific routes in cities. In most of the state, cycle rickshaws, and in Kolkata, hand-pulled rickshaws, are also used for short-distance travel.

Netaji Subhash Chandra Bose International Airport is a hub for flights to and from Bangladesh, East Asia, Nepal, Bhutan, and Northeast India.

Durgapur Expressway

An SBSTC bus in Karunamoyee

Kolkata Metro, the first metro rail system of India

As of 2011, the total length of surface road in West Bengal is over 92,023 kilometres (57,180 miles); national highways comprise 2,578 km (1,602 mi) and state highways 2,393 km (1,487 mi). As of 2006, the road density of the state is 103.69 kilometres per square kilometre (166.87 miles per square mile), higher than the national average of 74.7 km/km^2(120.2 mi/sq mi).

As of 2011, the total railway route length is around 4,481 km (2,784 mi). Kolkata is the headquarters of three zones of the Indian Railways – Eastern Railway and South Eastern Railway, and the Kolkata Metro, which is the newly formed 17th zone of the Indian Railways. The Northeast Frontier Railway (NFR) serves the northern parts of the state. The Kolkata metro is the country's first underground railway. The Darjeeling Himalayan Railway, part of NFR, is a UNESCO World Heritage Site.

Netaji Subhas Chandra Bose International Airport at Dum Dum, Kolkata, is the state's biggest airport. Bagdogra Airport near Siliguri is a customs airport that offers international service to Bhutan and Thailand, besides regular domestic service. Kazi Nazrul Islam Airport, India's first private sector airport, serves the twin cities of Asansol-Durgapur at Andal, Bardhaman.

Kolkata is a major river port in eastern India. The Kolkata Port Trust manages the Kolkata and the Haldia docks. There is passenger service to Port Blair on the Andaman and Nicobar Islands and cargo ship service to ports in India and abroad, operated by the Shipping Corporation of India. Ferries are a principal mode of transport in the southern part of the state, especially in the Sundarbans area. Kolkata is the only city in India to have trams as a mode of transport, and these are operated by the Calcutta Tramways Company.

Several government-owned organisations operate bus services in the state, including the Calcutta State Transport Corporation, the North Bengal State Transport Corporation, the South Bengal State Transport Corporation, the West Bengal

Surface Transport Corporation, and the Calcutta Tramways Company.

There are also private bus companies. The railway system is a nationalised service without any private investment. Hired forms of transport include metered taxis and auto rickshaws, which often ply specific routes in cities.

In most of the state, cycle rickshaws, and in Kolkata, hand-pulled rickshaws and electric rickshaws, are used for short-distance travel.

PHYSICAL INFRASTRUCTURE DEVELOPMENT

Better Infrastructure = Bigger Investments

Keeping this major factor in mind, the state Government has laid great emphasis on strengthening existing and building new infrastructure to encourage more investments. The State offers a relatively developed physical and social infrastructure that has become instrumental in attracting the attention of investors both domestic as well as international. In order to develop, upgrade and maintain infrastructure facilities, the Government of West Bengal recognises and encourages Public-Private partnerships.

Roads

Connecting Bengal to the World...

The state of West Bengal is served by 92,023 km of roads within which, the National Highways cover a span of 2578 kms and State Highways 2,393 Km. The road density is 1.04 km per sq km, which is considerably higher than the national average of 0.75 km. Keeping in mind the need for speed and quality in connectivity and a vehicle population that is growing at over 11% per annum, the GoWB has taken up an ambitious infrastructure renewal and expansion program

Some of the key initiatives in the roads sector are:

The North South Economic Order developed with the support of ADB at a cost of US$ 210 million with a view to link the southern ports of Haldia and Kolkata with the northern hinterland of the State.

The North South Corridor

Dankuni - Kolaghat, Dankuni – Kharagpur National Highway project. Vivekananda Bridge which is an approach to NH2 has been completed.

Four laning of NH41 from Kolkaghat to Haldia, NH31 passing through North Bengal, NH117 from Kona to Netaji Subhas Docks, NH35 from Barasat to Petrapole and NH31 from Kolkata to Dalkhola.

The State Government has also taken up Eastern link Highway project (100km) connecting Barasat to Raichak.

31 km long State Highway linking NH31 from Siliguri to Jalpaiguri via Falakata to be upgraded to National Highway

Some major stretches of the Golden Quadrilateral project undertaken by the National Highway Authority of India (NHAI) will pass through major North Bengal Districts.

Entire stretch of roads connecting Bengal with the North Eastern States and Bihar has been strengthened and improved.

Entire stretch of NH2 connecting Kolkata to New Delhi is being widened to 4 lanes. The Durgapur and Kona Expressways are fully operational and provide easier access to Kolkata from NH2

Under the Jawaharlal Nehru National Urban Renewal Mission, the State Government has taken the initiative to come up with a Rs. 27 billion action plan which includes extension and widening of arterial roads, widening and strengthening of secondary roads, construction of pedestrian underpasses, bridges, flyovers, elevated roads, traffic and transportation systems including modern passenger dispersal systems. Several foreign companies are already in the fray to partner the GoWB in its efforts for improvement of roads. Indonesia based Salim Group would be constructing the Eastern Link Highway from Barasat to Raichak, and two Four Lane Road Bridges across the

Hooghly and Haldi rivers facilitating connectivity between Kolkata and the port city of Haldia.

Railways

West Bengal is well connected by 4154.98 km of railway tracks of which some 2227.73 km run on electricity.

The East West Metro Corridor Project connecting Salt Lake to Howrah is already under implementation. The state Government is also considering the extension of East-West Metro from Salt Lake to NSC Bose Airport

Airways

Kolkata is well connected to the rest of India and all other prime locations of the world by the Netaji Subhas Chandra Bose International Airport. Kolkata Airport had international traffic of 1.01 million and domestic traffic of 6.45 million in 2007-08. Currently, the Kolkata International Airport is being modernized with an investment of US$ 30 million, which includes the development of a new integrated cargo complex. There is another airport at Bagdogra, which links Siliguri with the important destinations within the country. The importance of Bagdogra airport has increased with Siliguri becoming the gateway to North Eastern States and a vital trade and logistics hub for the entire region. The State Government has set up a perishable goods cargo complex at Bagdogra airport. The State Government is actively engaged in making the existing airport at Cooch Behar fully operational with the help of the Airports Authority of India.

Inland Waterways

The Government of India has declared the entire stretch of Ganges between Haldia and Allahabad as National Waterway (NW1). The 560 km Haldia – Farakka stretch of NW1 in West Bengal will be developed as a part of the multi modal system for cargo tariff from Nepal, Bhutan, North Bengal & North Eastern States.

The Transport Department, GoWB has initiated plans to reclaim the North Canal system, a 43 kms stretch of canal that stretches from the river Hooghly right across to the river Raimangal on the Bangladesh border. This was once the artery of trade which can restore trade links and lead to substantial economic development of the region.

Ports

The state of West Bengal has two modern ports – Kolkata and Haldia which together handled 54.22 million tonnes of cargo in 2008-09. During 2008-09, Kolkata Port ranked 'fifth' amongst all Indian major ports in terms of cargo handling. Currently both ports are being modernized and upgraded to cope with the growth in cargo.

An outlay of US$ 222.26 million has been projected in the 11th Plan for Kolkata Port Trust. The outlay for Kolkata Dock System is in tune of US$ 45.17 million and that of Haldia Dock Complex is US$ 83.15 million.

In addition, a new 3000 acre port-cum-Special Economic Zone is coming up in Kulpi in collaboration with Dubai based DP World. The process of setting up a Deep Sea Port near Kolkata has been initiated by the Ministry of Shipping, Government of India. Recently a deep-sea fishing harbour has been approved which will increase the export of marine fish and fish products to over 25,000 tonnes per year.

Kolkata Dock System (KDS) handled traffic of 12.428 million tonnes in 2008-2009 as against 13.741 million tonnes in 2007-2008. At Haldia Dock Complex (HDC), 41.792 million tonnes of traffic was handled in 2008-2009 as against 43.588 million tonnes in 2007-2008.

During the last nine-year period, from 2000-2001 to 2008-2009, Kolkata Port increased its cargo volume by 24.22 million tonnes (80.73%).

The Inland Water Traffic at KDS increased to 10.69 lakh tonnes in 2007-08 from 8.63 lakh tonnes in 2006-07, i.e. a growth of 23.87% was registered.

Sea board traffic handled by the two ports in the year 2007 - 2008 was 57.482 million tonnes.

Power

West Bengal has been a pioneer in power development over the years. NASSCOM-Gartner ranks West Bengal's power infrastructure as the best in the country. There has been an installed capacity of 9629.9 MW in the State in 2008-09.

Power Generation in the State is handled by various units – The West Bengal State Electricity Board, the West Bengal Power Development Corporation Ltd. and Durgapur Projects Ltd. (State Sector); Damodar Valley Corporation and the National Thermal Power Corporation (Central Sector); and the Calcutta Electric Supply Company and Dishergarh Power Supply Company (Private Sector). Electricity Generation in the State is in tune of 47471.9 million units. During the 12th five year plan 3350 MW is likely to be added in the state power sector through new projects to be undertaken by WBPDCL, DPL and CESC. Besides these, the proposed green field steel/ aluminium plants are likely to add substantial capacity in the power sector as captive source of their plants. Steps have been taken by most of the power generating agencies for addition of significant capacity of 4570 MW by 2010-11/2011-12.The state government is encouraging setting up of renewable energy based power plants and around 60 MW capacity is likely to be added in the renewable energy sector by 2009-10.

Communication Infrastructure

Kolkata, the state's capital offers more than 580 Mbps of international satellite connectivity through VSNL & 5 STPI Earth Stations at Kolkata, Durgapur, Kharagpur, Haldia and Siliguri. Cable connectivity is provided through leased BSNL lines to Mumbai & onward connectivity through submarine cables. Besides BSNL, private players like Reliance Infocomm, Vodafone & Bharti Airtel also connect Kolkata to the rest of the world. A submarine cable landing station is likely to be set up at Digha. The State considers IT a basic mission that can help the people uplift their standard of living. The Government of West Bengal has adopted measures to spread IT infrastructure right across the state. Reliance Group has set up a well spread out Optical Fibre Cable network in the State, which is a part of their National Broadband Access Project.

The BSNL optical fibre network extends over 15,000 route kilometers and has ensured connectivity on demand even at the block level. This has facilitated e-governance, telemedicine, and wide connectivity throughout the state. Connectivity upto block level has been established in all nineteen districts. The BSNL optical fibre network has ensured connectivity at the block level.The cellular network has made spectacular inroads into the state. The state as a whole had 27.22 million mobile subscribers during 2008-09 as against 17.22 million in 2007-08 registering an increase by 58%.The share of West Bengal mobile subscribers on an all India basis stood at 6.9% during 2008-09 as against 6.6% during 2007-08.

7

Tourism

Tourism in West Bengal refers to West Bengal's tourism. West Bengal is a state in the eastern region of India and is the nation's fourth-most populous.The state capital is Kolkata (formerly *Calcutta*). The state encompasses two broad natural regions: the Gangetic Plain in the south and the sub-Himalayan and Himalayan area in the north. The tourism in West Bengal is maintained by WBTDCL, a state government owned enterprise.

West Bengal, located on eastern bottleneck of India stretching from the Himalayas in the north to the Bay of Bengal in the south, presents some of marvelous landscape features and natural scenic beauty. Some of India's most preferred travel destinations like; the Darjeeling Himalayan hill region in the northern extreme of the state, the highest peak of the state Sandakphu (3,636 m or 11,929 ft) and the Sundarbans mangrove forests in the extreme south.

During the British colonial era from 1700–1912, Kolkata enjoyed the privilege of being the capital of British India and witnessed a spate of frenzied construction of buildings, largely influenced by the conscious intermingling of Neo-Gothic, Baroque, Neo-Classical, Oriental and Islamic schools of design. Unlike many north Indian cities, whose construction stresses minimalism, the layout of much of the architectural variety in Kolkata owes its origins to European styles and tastes imported by the British and, to a much lesser extent, by the Portuguese and French.

Currently Bollywood star Shah Rukh Khan is the brand ambassador of West Bengal Tourism. The promotional films on West Bengal starring Shah Rukh Khan have been directed by Indian National Award winning filmmaker Aniruddha Roy Chowdhury.

Architectural and geographical

Howrah Bridge

The state of West Bengal has significant architectural and natural heritage. The capital of the state, Kolkata is also known as the "City of Palaces". West Bengal is famous for its terracotta temples of Bishnupur.

Hazarduari Palace, a popular tourist attraction, is known to have the second largest chandelier in the world and also the largest staircase in India. This three-storey palace was built in 1837 by Duncan McLeod for Nawab Nazim Humaun Jah, the then Nawab of Bengal. The palace was built in the Indo-European style. It derives its name from the thousand doors in the palace (among which only 900 are real). In 1985, the palace was handed over to the Archaeological Survey of India (ASI) for better preservation. The Hazarduari Palace Museum is regarded as the biggest site museum of ASI and has 20 displayed galleries containing 4742 antiquities, 1034 of which are displayed for the public. They include various weapons, oil paintings of Dutch, French and Italian artists, marble statues, rare books, old maps, land revenue records, and palanquins(mostly belonging to 18th and 19th centuries). Cooch Behar Palace built in 1887, was designed on the model of Buckingham Palace in London, during the reign of Maharaja Nripendra Narayan.

The Victoria Memorial, Howrah Bridge (*Rabindra Setu*) and the Second Hooghly Bridge (*Vidyasagar Setu*) are iconic of Kolkata. Aside from colonial and heritage buildings, there are also high rising monuments and skyscrapers in the city. There are also a couple of cemeteries established by the British when Kolkata was the capital of British India. These include the South Park Street Cemetery and Scottish Cemetery.

The River Ganga flows through the state. World heritage sites in West Bengal include the Darjeeling Himalayan Railwayand the Sundarbans National Park. Neora Valley National Park, which is one of the richest biological zones in the entire Northeast, situated in the Kalimpong subdivision under Darjeeling District, is in West Bengal.

The Ganges Delta (also known as the Ganges–Brahmaputra Delta, the Sunderbans Delta, or the Bengalla Delta) is in the South Asia region of Bengal, consisting of West Bengal and its neighbouring country of Bangladesh. It is the world's largest delta, and empties into the Bay of Bengal. It is one of the most fertile regions in the world, thus earning the nickname "The Green Delta". It stretches from the Hooghly River on the west to the Meghna River on the east. It is approximately 350 km (220 mi) across at the Bay of Bengal. Kolkata and Haldia are the principal Indian seaports on the delta.

The Acharya Jagadish Chandra Bose Indian Botanic Garden or Calcutta Botanical Garden (previously known as Indian

Botanic Garden) is the largest and oldest reserve of greeneries of its kind in South East Asia. It is also a premier institution for botanical and horticultural research in India. The garden is situated on the west bank of the River Hooghly in Shibpur, Howrah, nearly 8 km from center of city Kolkata. Located here is the Great Banyan Tree. It was the widest tree in the world in terms of the area of its canopy and is estimated to be about 200 to 250 years old. It became diseased after it was struck by lightning, so in 1925 the middle of the tree was excised to keep the remainder healthy.

West Bengal also has some more geographical indications like Nakshi Kantha(handicraft), Darjeeling tea (agricultural), *Santipore* saree (handicraft), Shantiniketan leather goods (handicraft), Fazli mango (agricultural), Khirsapati or *Himsagar* mango (agricultural), *Laxman Bhog* mango (agricultural), *Baluchari* saree (handicraft), and *Dhaniakhali* saree (handicraft).

Sea beaches

West Bengal stretches to the Bay of Bengal in the south. The coastal strip of West Bengal, extending from the Gangetic Delta to the border of Orissa, has some beautiful coastal settlements, such as Digha, Shankarpur, Mandarmani, Bakkhali, Gangasagara, and Tajpur. Some of these have beaches which are hard enough for cars to drive on.

Hill stations

There are many hill stations in North West Bengal, of which Darjeeling is world-famous. Others are Kurseong, Kalimpong, Rimbick, Lava and Loleygaon, Mirik and Sandakfu.

Wildlife sanctuaries and national parks

West Bengal has 3.26% of its geographical area under protected areas comprising 15 wildlife sanctuaries and 5 national parks — Sundarbans National Park, Buxa Tiger Reserve, Gorumara National Park, Neora Valley National Park, Singalila National Park, and Jaldapara National Park. West Bengal also has wildlife sanctuaries and bird sanctuaries like Chintamani Kar Bird Sanctuary and Raiganj Wildlife Sanctuary.

Flora and fauna

As of 2009, recorded forest area in the state is 11,879 km (4,587 sq mi) which is 13.38% of the state's geographical area, compared to the national average of 21.02%. Part of the world's largest mangrove forest, the Sundarbans, is located in southern West Bengal.

The southern part of West Bengal can be divided into two regions: the Gangetic plain and the littoral mangrove forests of the Sundarbans. The coastal region of Purba Medinipur exhibits coastal vegetation. A notable tree from the Sundarbans is the ubiquitous *sundari* (*Heritiera fomes*), from which the forest gets its name.

The distribution of vegetation in northern West Bengal is dictated by elevation and precipitation. For example, the foothills of the Himalayas, the *Dooars*, are densely wooded with Sal and other tropical evergreen trees. However, above an elevation of 1,000 metres (3,300 ft), the forest becomes predominantly subtropical. In Darjeeling, which is above 1,500 metres (4,900 ft), temperate-forest trees such as oaks, conifers, and rhododendrons predominate.

Wildlife include Indian rhinoceros, Indian elephant, deer, bison, leopard, gaur, tiger, and crocodiles, as well as many bird species. Migratory birds come to the state during the winter. The high-altitude forests of Singalila National Park shelter barking deer, red panda, chinkara, takin, serow, pangolin, minivet and Kalij pheasants. The Sundarbans are noted for a reserve project conserving the endangered Bengal tiger, although the forest hosts many other endangered species, such as the Gangetic dolphin, river terrapin and estuarine crocodile. The mangrove forest also acts as a natural fish nursery, supporting coastal fishes along the Bay of Bengal. Recognizing its special conservation value, Sundarban area has been declared as a Biosphere Reserve.

Culture

The culture of West Bengal attracts tourists from around the world. It has its roots in literature, music, fine arts, drama and cinema. The Darjeeling Himalayan hill regionshows a different cultural aspect. Rabindranath Tagore is Asia's first Nobel laureate and composer of India's national anthem. Swami Vivekananda was a key figure in introducing Vedanta and Yoga in Europe and the USA. They all belong from West Bengal, and their houses and residencies like Shantiniketan and Jorasanko Thakur Bari are world-famous and attract many tourists.

West Bengal also has a long tradition of popular literature, music and drama largely based on Bengali folklore and Hindu epics and Puranas.

The Baul tradition is a unique heritage of Bengali folk music, which has also been influenced by regional music traditions.Other folk music forms include Gombhira and Bhawaiya. Folk music in West Bengal is often accompanied by the ektara, a one-stringed instrument. West Bengal also has an heritage in North Indian classical music. "Rabindrasangeet", songs composed and set into tune by Rabindranath Tagore, and "Nazrul geeti" (by Kazi Nazrul Islam) are popular. Also prominent are other musical forms like Dwijendralal, Atulprasad and Rajanikanta's songs, and *"adhunik"* or modern music from films and other composers.

However, since the early 1990s, there has been an emergence and popularisation of new genres of music, including fusions of Baul and jazz by several Bangla bands, as well as the emergence of *Jeebonmukhi Gaan* (a modern genre based on realism). Bengali dance forms draw from folk traditions, especially those of the tribal groups, as well as the broader Indian dance traditions. Chau dance of Purulia is a rare form of mask dance. West Bengal is known for Bengali folk music such as baul and kirtans and *gajan*, and modern songs including Bengali "*adhunik*" (modern) songs.

The state is home to a thriving cinema industry, dubbed

"Tollywood". Tollygunje in Kolkata is the location of numerous Bengali movie studios, and the name "Tollywood" (similar to Hollywood and Bollywood) is derived from that name. The Bengali film industry is well known for its art films, and has produced acclaimed directors like Satyajit Ray and actors like Uttam Kumar and singers like Arijit Singh.

Among other types of theatre, West Bengal has a tradition of folk drama known as *jatra.*

West Bengal has been the harbinger of modernism in fine arts.

Kolkata was also the workplace of several social reformers, like Raja Ram Mohan Ray, Iswar Chandra Vidyasagar, and Swami Vivekananda. These social reforms have eventually led to a cultural atmosphere where practices like sati, dowry, and caste-based discrimination or untouchability, the evils that crept into the Hindu society, were abolished.

Kumortuli is a famous tourist attraction in Kolkata. It is traditionally a potters' quarter in North Kolkata. By virtue of their artistic productions these potters have moved from obscurity to prominence. This Kolkata neighbourhood not only supplies clay idols of Hindu gods and goddesses to *barowari pujas* in Kolkata and its neighbourhoods, but also exports a number of idols. It is one of the seven wonders in Kolkata. Bengal is also well known for its variety of handwoven Sarees. It is home to exquisite sarees such as Jamdani Sarees, Baluchari Sarees, Kantha stitch Sarees, Tussar Silk Sarees, Muslin Sarees and Matka Sarees. These variety of handwoven sarees in a single place is a rarity in today's modern times.

Cuisine

Rice and fish are traditional favourite foods, leading to a saying in Bengali, *machhe bhate bangali,* that translates as "fish and rice make a Bengali". Bengal's vast repertoire of fish-based dishes includes hilsa preparations, a favourite among Bengalis. There are numerous ways of cooking fish depending on the texture, size, fat content and bones.

Sweets occupy an important place in the diet of Bengalis and at their social ceremonies. It is an ancient custom among both Hindu and Muslim Bengalis to distribute sweets during festivities.

The confectionery industry has flourished because of its close association with social and religious ceremonies. Competition and changing tastes have helped to create many new sweets. Bengalis make distinctive sweetmeats from milk products, including *rôshogolla*, *chômchôm*, *kalojam* and several kinds of *sondesh*. Pitha, a kind of sweet cake, bread or dim sum are specialties of winter season. Sweets like coconut-naru, til-naru, moa, and payesh are prepared during the festival of Lakshmi puja. Popular street food includes *aloor chop*, beguni, kati roll, and phuchka.

Darjeeling Himalayan Hill Region

Apart from the major Hindu religious festivals like Diwali, Christmas, Dussera, Holi, Ram Navami, the diverse ethnic populace of Darjeeling Himalayan hill region celebrates several local festivals. The Tibetan ethnic groups like the Lepchas, Bhutias, Gurungs, and Tamangs celebrate new year called Losar in January/February, Maghe Sankranti, Chotrul Duchen, Buddha Jayanti, and Tendong Lho Rumfaat, to name a few, which provide the "regional distinctness" of Darjeeling's local culture from the rest of West Bengal.

A popular food in Darjeeling is the *momo*, a steamed dumpling containing either mutton, pork, beef or vegetables cooked in a doughy wrapping served with a watery vegetable soup and spicy tomato sauce/chutney. Wai-Wai is a favourite packaged snack of Darjeeling hills comprising noodles which are eaten either dry or with soup. *Churpee*, a kind of hard cheese made from cow or yak's milk, is another popular mini-snack that is both nutritious and a pastime. A form of noodle called *thukpa*, served with soup and vegetables, is extremely popular in and around the hills of Darjeeling. *Chhang* and *tongba* are local alcoholic beverages made from millet.

Pilgrimages

West Bengal attracts tourists for pilgrimages to the holy places of different religions.

Hinduism

Face of the idol of Goddess Bhavatarini from the Dakshineshwar Kali Temple

People from different sections of the world come to West Bengal for holy pilgrimages as Kolkata is one of the four *adiShaktipeethas*. Among the other 52 *shaktipeethas*, some are located in West Bengal. They are as follows:

- Bardhaman
- Bahula, on the banks of Ajay River at Ketugram, 8 km from Katwa, Burdwan, West Bengal
- Ujaani, 16 km from Guskara station under Burdwan district of West Bengal
- A temple locally known as *Bhramari Devi*, behind a rice mill, near Jalpesh Temple in Jalpaiguri, West Bengal

- *Yoga Adya* at Khirgram; under Burdwan district, West Bengal
- Kalighat Kalipeeth in Kolkata
- Kireet at Kireetkona village, 3 km from Lalbag Court Road station under Murshidabad district, West Bengal
- Kankalitala, on the banks of Kopai River 10 km north-east of Bolpur station in Birbhum district. Devi locally known as Kankaleshwari.
- Vibhash, at Tamluk, under district Purba Medinipur, West Bengal
- Tarapith

Only one *Maha Shaktipeethas*, known as Pradyumna, existed. This temple is currently non-existent. Only ruins are found in these places. Instead, Sringeri in Karnataka is believed to be the Shakti Peeth of this aspect of the Goddess. Other than the *shaktipeethas* many other famous temples also exist. They are the famous Belur Math, Mayapur ISKCON Temple, Hangseshwari Temple, Tarakeshwar Temple, Thakurnagar Thakur Ari Temple and Dakshineswar Kali Temple.

Jainism

- Pakbirra Jain temple, Purulia
- Calcutta Jain Temple, Kolkata
- Shree Digambar Jain Pareswanath Temple, Belgachia
- Sat Deul
- Harmasra Jain temple

Islam

There are countless mosques in West Bengal but some of them are very famous like the *Nizamat Imambara* in Murshidabad, Katra Mosque which is also in Murshidabad, Furfura Sharif and Tipu Sultan Shahi Mosque on Jawaharlal Nehru Road in Kolkata.

Sikhism

There are many Gurudwaras in West Bengal like Gurudwara

Bari Sangat in Kolkata, Gurudwara Chhoti Sangat, Gurudwara Nima Serai Sri Guru Tegh Bahadur, Gurudwara Sikh Sangat and Gurudwara Liluah Belur Sikh Sangat in Liluah.

Christianism

There are also many churches in West Bengal like the Basilica of the Holy Rosary in Bandel, St. John's Church, St. Jame's Church (*Jora Girja*), St. Paul's Cathedral and Church of the Lord Jesus.

Buddhism

There are also many Buddhist monasteries in West Bengal, especially in the hilly regions, like the Ghoom Monastery, Bhutia Busty Monastery, Mag-Dhog Yolmowa Monastery, Tharpa Choling Monastery, and Zang Dhok Palri Phodang.

Seven wonders of West Bengal

NDTV along with the Ministry of Tourism, Government of India, conducted a nationwide campaign for searching the "Seven Wonders of India" in 2008-09. The campaign started with shortlisting 200 places from all of the Indian states and then inviting the public to cast their vote for their favourites. It also included seven wonders of particular states. In West Bengal a total 13 were selected of which the "Seven Wonders of West Bengal" were shortlisted. The list of the 30 selected places are as follows:

- Cooch Behar Palace
- Darjeeling Himalayan Railway ("Toy Train")
- Hazarduari Palace
- Adina Mosque
- Gaur, West Bengal
- Shantiniketan
- Bishnupur Terracotta Temples
- Acharya Jagadish Chandra Bose Indian Botanic Garden with the Great Banyan Tree

- Howrah Bridge
- B. B. D. Bagh (formerly called Dalhousie Square)
- Dakshineswar Kali Temple
- Second Hooghly Bridge
- Victoria Memorial
- Sunderbans
- St. Paul's Cathedral

The shortlisted list, compiling of the "Seven Wonders of West Bengal" as per the votings is as follows:

- Sunderbans
- Victoria Memorial
- Darjeeling Himalayan Railway ("Toy Train")
- Bishnupur Terracotta Temples
- Acharya Jagadish Chandra Bose Indian Botanic Garden with the Great Banyan Tree
- Howrah Bridge
- B. B. D. Bagh (formerly called the Dalhousie Square)

SUNDARBANS NATIONAL PARK

The Sundarbans National Park is a National Park, Tiger Reserve, UNESCO World Heritage Site and a Biosphere Reserve located in the Sundarbans delta in Indian state of West Bengal. This region is densely covered by mangrove forests, and is one of the largest reserves of the Bengal tiger. It is also home to a variety of bird, reptile and invertebrate species, including the salt-water crocodile.

Origin: Sundarbans National Park got its name from the local mangrove sundari trees which are found in abundance throughout the park.

History: The present Sundarbans National Park was declared as the core area of Sundarbans Tiger Reserve in 1973 and a wildlife sanctuary in the year 1977. On 4 May 1984 it was declared a National Park. It was given a world heritage site in the year 1985. Whole Sundarbans area was declared as Biosphere Reserve in 1989.

Geography: Sundarbans National Park is located in between 30° 24' - 30° 28' N longitude and between 77° 40' - 77° 44' E latitude in the South 24 Parganas district in the Indian state of West Bengal. The average altitude of the park is 7.5 m above sea level. The park is made up of 54 small islands and it crisscrossed by several tributaries of Ganga and Brahmaputra.

Sundarbans National Park is the largest estuarine mangrove forest in the world. Twenty-six of the fifty broad mangrove types found in the world grow well in the Sundarbans. The commonly identifiable vegetation that grow in the dense mangrove forests at the Sundarbans are salt water mixed forest, mangrove scrub, brackish water mixed forest, littoral forest, wet forest and wet alluvial grass forests.

Climate: The average maximum and minimum temperature is 34 °C and 20 °C respectively. Rainfall is heavy with high humidity as high as 80% as it is close to the Bay of Bengal. The monsoon lasts from mid-June to mid-September. Prevailing wind is from the north and north-east from October to mid-March and south west westerlies prevails from mid-March to September. Storms which sometimes develop into cyclones are common during the month of May and October.

Flora and Fauna: There are 64 plant species in Sundarbans and they have the capacity to withstand estuarine conditions and saline inundation on account of tidal effects. In the month of April and May the flaming red leaves of the Genwa the crab-like red flowers of the Kankara and the yellow flowers of Khalsi can be seen, which add a beauty to the surroundings. Some of the more commonly found plants and trees in the park are Genwa, Dhundal, Passur, Garjan, Kankra, Sundari and Goran.

The Sundarbans forest is home to more than 200 tigers. The Royal Bengal Tigers have developed a unique characteristic of swimming in the saline waters, and are world famous for their man-eating tendencies.

Apart from the Royal Bengal Tiger; Fishing Cats, Macaques, Wild Boar, Common Grey Mongoose, Fox, Jungle Cat, Flying

Fox, Pangolin, Chital, are also found in abundance in the Sundarbans.

Avifauna: Some of the more popular birds found in this region are - Open Billed Storks, White Ibis, Water Hens, Coots, Pheasant Tailed Jacanas, Pariah Kites, Brahminy Kites, Marsh Harriers, Swamp Partridges, Red Jungle Fowls, Spotted Doves, Common Mynahs, Jungle Crows, Jungle Babblers, Cotton Teals, Herring Gulls, Caspian Terns, Gray Herons, Brahminy Ducks, Spotted Billed Pelicans, Large Egrets, Night Herons, Common Snipes, Wood Sandpipers, Green Pigeons, Rose Ringed Parakeets, Paradise Flycatchers, Cormorants, Fishing Eagles, White Bellied Sea Eagles, Seagulls, Common Kingfishers, Peregrine falcons, Woodpeckers, Whimprels, Black-Tailed Godwits, Little Stints, Eastern Knots, Curlews, Golden Plovers, Pintails, White Eyed Pochards and Whistling Teals.

Aqua Fauna: Some of the fish and amphibians found in the park are Saw Fish, Butter Fish, Electric Rays, Silver Carp, Star Fish, Common Carp, King Crabs, Prawn, Shrimps, Gangetic Dolphins, Skipping Frogs, Common Toads and Tree Frogs.

Reptiles: The Sundarbans National Park houses an excellent number of reptiles as well. Some of the common ones are - Olive Ridley Turtles, Sea Snakes, Dog Faced Water Snakes, Green Turtles, Estuarine Crocodiles, Chameleons, King Cobras, Salvator Lizards, Hard Shelled Batgun Terrapins, Russels Vipers, Mouse Ghekos, Monitor Lizards, Curviers, Hawks Bill Turtles, Pythons, Common Kraits, Chequered Killbacks and rat Snakes.

Endangered Species: The endangered species that lives within the Sundarbans are Royal Bengal Tiger, Estuarian Crocodile, River Terrapin (Batagur baska), Olive Ridley Turtle, Gangetic Dolphin, Ground Turtle, Hawks Bill Turtle and King Crabs (Horse shoe).

Management and Special Projects

The park has got protection since its creation. The core area is free from all human disturbances like collection of wood, honey, fishing and other forest produces. However in buffer area fishing, honey collection and wood cutting are permitted in limited form. Protection of the park from poaching and theft of forest products is done by well armed forest staffs who patrols in motorboats and launches. Moreover forest offices and camps are located at several important parts of the park. Anti-poaching camps are manned by 2 to 3 knowledgeable labourers under supervision of concerned beat guard/Forester/Range officer.

Habitat of wildlife is well maintained through eco-conservation, eco-development, training, education and research. 10 Forest Protection Committees and 14 Eco-development Committees have been formed in the fringe of Sundarbans Tiger Reserve helps in this regard. Seminars, workshops, awareness camps, etc. are organised frequently in the vicinity of park to educate the people on eco-conservation, eco-development and such other issues. Mangrove and other plants are planted in the fringe area to meet the local need of fuel wood for about 1000 villages and to conserve the buffer area. Conservation of soil is done to maintain the ecological balance. Several sweet water ponds have been dug up inside the park to provide drinking water to the wild animals.

Controlling man-eating tigers is another major activity. The number of causalities has been reduced from 40 to 10 per year. The reduction in number of causalities is a result of strict control over the movement of the people inside the tiger reserve, alternative income generation and awareness building among people. It is also believed that due to use of human masks and electric human dummies. Straying of tigers into nearby villages is prevented through effective measures like nylon net fencing, solar illumination of villages, etc. The youths of the villages are given training in controlling the straying of tigers into the villages.

The Mangrove Interpretation Centre is established at Sajnekhali to make the local people and tourists aware about importance of conservation of nature in general and specially the mangrove eco-systems.

Constraints: Though there is tough protection in the park there are a few loopholes. The geographical topography with hostile terrain criss-crossed by several rivers and their tributaries, long international border with Bangladesh, fishing trawlers and launches helps in poaching, cutting of wood and also affecting the mangrove forests. Lack of staffs, infrastructure and lack of funds also added up the factors.

Park-specific Information

Activities: The best and only means of travelling the park is to hire a boat and float down the various lanes formed by the many flowing rivers. You can travel in any of the local boats or in luxury launches namely M.V. *Chitrarekha* and M. V. *Madhukar*, which are operated by the tourism department.

Apart from viewing the wildlife from the boat safaris, you can also visit the following places in Sundarbans which are Bhagatpur Crocodile Project which is a crocodile breeding farm (access from Namkhana), Sagar Island, Jambudweep, Sudhanyakali watchtower, Buriidabri Tiger Project, Netidhopani Watchtower, Haliday Island (famous for Barking Deer), Kanak (nesting place of Olive Ridley Turtle), Sajankhali Bird Sanctuary (famous for avian fauna).

Lodging: Forest lodge and forest rest-houses are available for accommodation at Sajnekhali, Bakkhali and Piyali. The cruise launches M.V. Chitralekha and M.V. Sarbajaya also have lodging facility.

Lodging facilities are also available at Sundarbans Jungle Camp on Bali Island run by Help Tourism Group with collaboration with local communities and members of Bali Nature and Wildlife Conservation Society.

Approach:

- Nearest airport: Dum Dum airport at Kolkata is 112 km away.
- Nearest railhead: Canning is 48 km away from the Park.
- Nearest Road: Road transportation is available from Kolkata for Namkhana (105 km), Sonakhali (100 km), Raidighi (76 km), Canning (64 km), and Najat (92 km), which are all

near the Sunderbans and have access to the riverine waterways.

- Nearest town: Gosaba is 50 km away.
- Nearest city: Kolkata which is 112 km away.

SINGALILA NATIONAL PARK

Singalila National Park is a national park of India located on the Singalila Ridge at an altitude of more than 7000 feet above sea level, in the Darjeeling district of West Bengal. It is well known for the trekking route to Sandakphu that runs through it.

History: The park was declared a Wildlife Sanctuary in 1986, and was made an Indian National Park in 1992. The region had long been used as the trekking route from [Manebhanjhyang] to Sandakphu (the highest peak of West Bengal), and Phalut.

Geography

Political Geography: The park is located in the Darjeeling subdivision, Darjeeling district, West Bengal, India. It is bordered on the north by the state of Sikkim and on the west by the country of Nepal.

Physical Geography: The park is part of the Eastern Himalayas. The Singalila Ridge, which runs roughly North to South and separates Himalayan West Bengal from the other Eastern Himalayan ranges to the west of it. The two highest peaks of West Bengal, Sandakphu (3630 m) and Phalut (3600 m) are located on the ridge and inside the park. River Rammam and River Sirikhola flow through the park.

Human History

The park has no significant history of human settlement. However, small settlements have grown up along the trekking route to Sandakphu and Phalut. There is a reasonably large village at Kala Pokhri, around the lake of the same name. The Singalila Ridge was used as an approach route by the first documented mountaineering team which unsuccessfully attempted to climb Kanchenjunga in 1905. The team was led by Jules Jacot-Guillarmod and the famous occultist Aleister Crowley.

Natural History

Biomes: The national park falls in the Indomalaya ecozone, and the biomes corresponding to the ecozone which are present in the park are :

- Eastern Himalayan subalpine conifer forests of the Temperate coniferous forests biome
- Eastern Himalayan broadleaf forests of the Temperate broadleaf and mixed forests biome
- Himalayan subtropical pine forests of the Subtropical coniferous forest biome

The subtropical biome roughly exists in the altitude range of 1800 m to 3000 m, and the temperate biome exists in the altitude range of 3000 m to 4500 m.

Flora and Fauna: Thick bamboo, oak, magnolia and rhododendron forest between 2000 and 3600 m cover the Singalila Ridge. There are two seasons of wildflower bloom- one in spring (March-April) when the Rhododendrons bloom, and another in the post-monsoon season (around October), when the lower forests bloom (Primula, Geranium, Saxifraga, Bistort, Senecio, Cotoneaster and numerous orchids). Sandakphu is known as the "mountain of poisonous plants" due to the large concentration of Himalayan Cobra Lilies (Arisaema) which grow there.

Mammals: The park has a number of small mammals including the Red Panda, Leopard Cat, Barking Deer, Yellow-throated Marten, Wild Boar, Pangolin and the Pika. Larger mammals include the Himalayan Black Bear, Leopard, Clouded Leopard, Serow and the Takin. Tigers occasionally wander into the area, but do not have a large enough prey base to make residence in these forests feasible.

Birds: The park is a birder's delight with over 120 species recorded including many rare and exotic species like the Scarlet Minivet, Kalij Pheasant, Blood Pheasant, Satyr Tragopan, Brown and Fulvous Parrotbills, Rufous-vented Tit, and Old World babblers like the Fire-tailed Myzornis and the Golden-breasted Fulvetta. The park is also on the flyway of many migratory birds.

Reptiles and Amphibians: The endangered Himalayan Newt frequents the region, and congregates around the lakes of Jore Pokhri, Sukhia Pokhri and nearby lakes to reproduce. Jore Pokhri and Sukhia Pokhri are within 20 km of the park boundary, and are protected wildlife sanctuaries.

Conservation Issues

The major issues at the park are trash collection on trekking routes and ensuring minimal damage of flora by trekkers, as flora at such high altitudes tend to grow really slowly. Grazing of yak and cattle from neighbouring villages can also be a problem. Forest fires can be a threat to the park, especially in Spring when the accumulated debris from winter can be a hazard. A forest fire swept through the national park on March 6, 2006.

Even though the national park has a resident Red Panda population of only about 20 - 25 members, Project Red Panda (funded by the Central Zoo Authority) chose Singalila National Park for reintroduction of Red Pandas from its captive breeding programme at the Padmaja Naidu Himalayan Zoological Park in Darjeeling, mainly due to reasons of proximity. Two females, Sweety and Milli, were released in November 2004. Milli was killed by a leopard, but Sweety adapted to the wild and gave birth to an offspring - the first such successful re-entry for Red Panda.

The reintroduction was filmed by noted Indian filmmakers Rajesh Bedi and Naresh Bedi. The documentary, named Cherub of the Mist, won the Best Conservation and Environmental Film at the 29th International Wildlife Film Festival in Montana.

Park-specific Information

The two seasons to visit the park are in Spring (March - May) and post Monsoon (mid September to early December). The park is closed to tourists from June 16 to September 15 every year on account of the monsoons.

Activities

Trekking and Camping: The trek along the Singalila Ridge to Sandakphu and Phalut is one of the most popular ones in the Eastern Himalayas, due to the grand vistas of the Kangchenjunga range, and the Everest range which can be seen from the ridge, and also for the seasonal wildflower blooms and birding. Treks begin at Manebhanjan which is 51 km (1.5 hrs by road) from Darjeeling. The trekking routes inside the National Park have 4 legs or stages.

- Manebhanjan to Meghma (2600 m): This is a 4 hour trek through the lower forest
- Meghma to Gairibans (2621 m): There are two alternative trekking routes. Both go via Tonglu (3070 m) and Tumling (2900 m). The boundary of the national park passes though Tomling and a checkpost is located there. From Tumling, a shorter trail cuts through Nepal and Jaubari (2750 m).
- Gairibans to Sandakphu (3636 m): This is a steep 4 hour climb up. Roughly half way up the climb is the village of Kala Pokhri (3186 m).
- Sandakphu to Phalut (3600 m): This is the most pristine stretch of the trek, offering great views of Kanchenjunga and Mt. Everest. It is a one day trek via Sabarkum (3536 m) covering 21 km. But the main problem of this sandakphu Phalut route is there is no water source in between so the trekker have to carry enough water to reach phalut.

The descent from Sandakphu can be accomplished in several ways:

- Retracing the way back to Manebhanjan

- A steep descent to the village of Sirikhola on the banks of the River Sirikhola, via Gurdum (2300 m), and from there to Rimbik.
- There is now a 4WD motorable road to Sandakphu, so one can hire a cab down to Manebhanjan and Darjeeling via Tomling and Tonglu if needed. The drive on the gravel road, however, is very arduous.

The descent from Phalut can also be accomplished in several ways:

- Retracing the way back to Manebhanjan
- A descent down to Sirikhola along high altitude meadows which have seasonal blooms. The descent is via Sabarkum and the abandoned village of Molley. A further trek leads one to the scenic village of Rimbik, which is motorable.
- The most popular descent is via the villages of Gorkey (on the banks of the River Rammam) and Samanden down to the village of Rammam. The trail then leads to Rimbik, and is shorter than the route via Sirikhola.

Birding: The Singalila National Park is one of the most popular birding spots in the Eastern Himalayas, since it attracts a large number of birds due to its seasonal blooms. Blooming seasons are the best times to see birds.

Lodging: Sailung Tea House is a small cozy place to stay while at Meghma. There are two roomed guest houses and trekkers' huts at Tonglu, Gairibans, Sandakphu, Phalut, Kala Pokhri and several other locations in the park, run by the Darjeeling Gorkha Hill Council. Numerous guest houses and lodging are available at Manebhanjan. The preferred way to visit the park is to stay in Darjeeling and camp inside the national park.

Approach:

- Nearest airport:
    - o Bagdogra Airport, Jalpaiguri district, West Bengal
    - o Gangtok Helipad, East Sikkim district, Sikkim
- Nearest railhead:

- o Narrow gauge: Ghum, West Bengal
- o Standard Gauge: New Jalpaiguri, West Bengal
- Nearest highway: NH 31A (Sivok - Gangtok) passes through Darjeeling (which is 1.5 hours by car from Manebhanjan)
- Nearest town: Manebhanjan—the access point for Rimbik and Tumling, the gateways to the park
- Nearest city: Darjeeling

KHOAI

Khoai refers to a geological formation specifically in Birbhum, Bardhaman, and Bankura districts of West Bengal, India and some parts of Jharkhand, India that is made up of laterite soil rich in iron oxide, often in the shapes of tiny hills.

The Khoai can only support certain types of plants. It is a very poor soil for most types of agriculture practiced in the areas in which it is found. Yet often, a khoai maybe situated adjacent to a naturally forested area.

Monsoon: A monsoon is a heavy rainy season which lasts for several months. The term was first used in English with this meaning in India, Bangladesh and neighbouring countries to mean the seasonal winds blowing from the Indian Ocean and Arabian Sea in the southwest bringing heavy rainfall to the region. It has come to be used in other tropical and subtropical regions with a stormy rainy season such as in North America, Sub-Saharan Africa and Brazil.

It was derived from the Hindi word *mausam* meaning 'weather' in the time of the British Empire. The Hindi word in turn was derived from the Arabic word *mausim* meaning 'season'.

Monsoon may also be used to mean the wind or a specific storm in the monsoon season having the typical direction and rainfall characteristics of that season.

In terms of total precipitation, total area covered and the total number of people affected, the monsoons affecting the Indian Subcontinent dwarfs the North American monsoon (also called the "Mexican", "southwest", "desert", or "Arizona" monsoon).

History: Strengthening of the Asian monsoon has been linked to the uplift of the Tibetan Plateau after the collision of India and Asia around 50 million years ago. Evidence for when this first happened remains controversial. Many geologists believe the monsoon first became strong around 8 million years ago based on records from the Arabian Sea and the record of wind-blown dust in the Loess Plateau of China.

More recently plant fossils in China and new long-duration sediment records from the South China Sea led Peter Clift to propose a much older monsoon starting around 24 million years ago and linked to early Tibetan uplift. Testing of this hypothesis awaits deep ocean sampling by the Integrated Ocean Drilling Programme. The monsoon has varied significantly in strength since this time, largely linked to global climate change, especially the cycle of the Pleistocene ice ages.

Processes: Monsoons are caused by the larger amplitude of the seasonal cycle of land temperature compared to that of nearby oceans. This differential warming happens because of the fact that heat in the ocean is mixed vertically through a "mixed layer" that may be fifty metres deep, through the action of wind and buoyancy-generated turbulence, whereas the land surface conducts heat slowly, with the seasonal signal penetrating perhaps a metre or so.

Additionally, the specific heat of liquid water is significantly higher than that of most materials that make up land. Together, these factors mean that the heat capacity of the layer participating in the seasonal cycle is much larger over the oceans than over land, with the consequence that land warms faster and reaches a higher temperature than the ocean. The hot air over the land tends to rise, creating an area of low pressure.

This creates a steady wind blowing toward the land, bringing the moist near-surface air over the oceans with it. Similar rainfall is caused by the moist ocean air being lifted upwards by mountains, surface heating, convergence at the surface, divergence aloft, or from storm-produced outflows at the surface. However the lifting occurs, the air cools due expansion in lower pressure, which in turn produces condensation.

In winter, the land cools off quickly, but the ocean keeps the heat longer. The hot air over the ocean rises, creating a low pressure area and a breeze from land to ocean while a large area of drying high pressure is formed over the land, increased by wintertime cooling. Monsoons are similar to sea breezes, a term usually referring to the localized, diurnal (daily) cycle of circulation near coastlines everywhere, but they are much larger in scale, stronger and seasonal.

Monsoon Systems: As monsoons have become better understood, the term monsoon has been broadened to include almost all of the phenomena associated with the annual weather cycle within the tropical and subtropical land regions of the earth.

Even more broadly, it is now understood that in the geological past, monsoon systems must have always accompanied the formation of supercontinents such as Pangaea, with their extreme continental climates.

Northeast Winter Monsoon (Asia)

In Asia, the northeastern winter monsoons take place from December to early March. The temperature over central Asia is lower, creating a zone of high pressure there. The jet stream in this region splits into the southern subtropical jet and the polar jet.

The subtropical flow directs northeasterly winds to blow across south Asia, creating dry air streams which produce clear skies over India from the months of November to May. Meanwhile, a low pressure system develops over northern Australia and winds are directed toward Australia known as a monsoon trough.

During the northeast winter monsoon, Australia and southeast Asia receive large amounts of rainfall.

Indian Ocean Monsoon

South-West Summer Monsoon: The southwestern summer monsoons occur from June to August. The Great Indian Desert (Thar Desert) and adjoining areas of the northern and central Indian Subcontinent heats up too much during the hot seasons of summer. This causes a low pressure area over the northern and central Indian subcontinent. To fill up this void, the moisture-laden winds from the Indian Ocean rush in to the subcontinent.

These winds, rich in moisture, are drawn towards the Himalayas, creating winds blowing storm clouds towards the subcontinent. However the Himalayas act like a high wall and do not allow the winds to pass into Central Asia, forcing them to rise. With the gain in altitude of the clouds, the temperature drops and precipitation occurs. Some areas of the subcontinent receive up to 10,000 mm of rain.

The southwest monsoon is generally expected to begin around the middle of June and dies down by September. The moisture-laden winds on reaching the southernmost point of the Indian peninsula, due to its topology, become divided into two parts:

- Arabian Sea Branch of the SW Monsoon
- Bay of Bengal Branch of the SW Monsoon

The Arabian Sea Branch of the SW Monsoon first hits the Western Ghats of the coastal state of Kerala, India and hence Kerela is the first state in India to receive rain from the South-West Monsoon. This branch of the monsoon moves northwards along the Western Ghats giving rain to the coastal areas west of the Western Ghats. It is to be noted that the eastern parts of the Western Ghats do not receive any rain from this monsoon as the wind does not cross the Western Ghats. The Bay of Bengal Branch of SW Monsoon flows over the Bay of Bengal heading towards North-Eastern India and Bengal, picking up more moisture from the Bay of Bengal. Its hits the Eastern Himalaya and provides a huge amount of rain to the regions of North-East India, Bangladesh and West Bengal. Cherripunji, situated on the southern slopes of the Eastern Himalaya in Shillong, India is one of the wettest place on Earth. After striking the Eastern Himalaya it turns towards the West, travels over the Indo-Gangetic Plain, at a rate of roughly 1-2 weeks per state, pouring raining all along its way.

The monsoon accounts for 80 percent of the rainfall in the country. Indian agriculture (which accounts for 25 percent of the GDP and employs 70 percent of the population) is heavily dependent on the rains, especially crops like cotton, rice, oilseeds and coarse grains. A delay of a few days in the arrival of the monsoon can, and does, badly affect the economy, as evidenced in the numerous droughts in India in the 90s. The monsoon is widely welcomed and appreciated by city-dwellers as well, for it provides relief from the climax of summer in June. However, because of the lack of adequate infrastructure in place, most major cities are often adversely affected as well. The roads, already shoddy, take a battering each year; houses and streets at the bottom of slopes and beside rivers are waterlogged, slums are flooded, and the sewers and the rare hurricane drain start to back up and pour out toxic filth rather than drain it away.

This translates into various minor casualties most of the time; lack of city infrastructure coupled with changing climate patterns also causes severe damage to and loss of property and life. Bangladesh and some regions of India like in Assam and places of West Bengal experiences heavy flood, which claims huge number of lives and huge loss of property and causes severe damage to economy, as evidenced in the Mumbai floods of 2005. Also in the recent past, areas in India that used to receive scanty rainfall throughout the year, like the Thar Desert, have surprisingly ended up receiving floods due to the prolonged monsoon season.

8

Population and Religion

POPULATION EXPLOSION IN WEST BENGAL

On account of the Partition of the Indian subcontinent in 1947, refugees moved from Pakistan, without much interruption, to various parts of India, especially to West Bengal, till 1971, when political boundaries in South Asia were redrawn. Even after the emergence of Bangladesh as an independent country in 1971, however, the march of refugees to West Bengal appeared to be ceaseless. Nevertheless, there is one great difference in the patterns of migration before and after 1971. In the days of Pakistan, nearly all refugees coming to West Bengal were members of the minority communities in East Bengal (East Pakistan), viz. Buddhists, Christians and Hindus.

In the Bangladesh era, however, in addition to the forced migration of members of minority community (the overwhelming majority being Hindus) to West Bengal, there has been large-scale voluntary infiltration of Bangladeshi Muslims (forming the majority community in that country) to West Bengal and other parts of India. Certainly, the Government of India and the Government of West Bengal are not unaware of this grim phenomenon. Occasionally, the Home Minister of the Government of India and the Chief Minister of West Bengal have expressed serious concern over this problem. This brief survey - its brevity attributable to the barrier of needless secrecy against the free flow of census data (unexpected in a democratic country like India) - aims at unravelling the mystery of population explosion in a progressive state like West Bengal, as also at arousing the consciousness of the public about the factor of migration /infiltration underlying this explosion, which cannot but pose a mounting challenge to vital national interests.

Table : Population in West Bengal 1941-91

Year	Population (100,000)	Increase of population in the previous decade (100,000)	Percentage rate of growth in the current decade
(1)	(2)	(3)	(4)
1941	232	43	22.9
1951	263	31	13.2
1961	349	86	32.8
1971	443	94	26.9
1981	546	103	23.2
1991	680	134	24.6

Source: Statistical Abstract, West Bengal, 1978-89 (Combined Issue), Bureau of Applied Economics and Statistics.

In accordance with estimates prepared by the Government of West Bengal, 44.5 lakhs of refugees came from East Bengal (East Pakistan) to West Bengal during 1946-1970. The 1981 Census contained an important clue to the persistence of migration / infiltration to West Bengal. The population growth rate declined from 26.9% in 1961-71 to 23.2% in 1971-81. Yet, the 1981 Census recorded a population of 4,67,000 in excess of the population derived from differences in birth /death rates. If one excluded these 4,67,000 persons - who obviously moved to West Bengal from other regions inside/outside India - the population growth rate in 1971-81 would have declined from 23.2% to 22.1%. Actually, in West Bengal, on account of an expansion of education and family planning programmes, as also of a pronounced rise in social consciousness, the population growth rate during 1981-91 should have fallen below 22%, and demographic experts of the Government of India perceptively forecast the rate of 20.79% for this period. Evidently, this forecast was upset by migration /infiltration from Bangladesh.

For, the 1991 Census puts the decadal growth rate at 24.55%, i.e. higher than that in 1971-81. Where and how could this unexpected rate of population growth take place?

Natural Population Increase in 1981-91: Every year the Registrar General of India conducts sample surveys, and estimates the annual rates of birth and death. Communicates these rates for West Bengal during 1981-90.

Table : Birth and Death Rates in West Bengal 1981-90

Year	Birth	Death	Natural increase of per thousand Population per Year
(1)	(2)	(3)	(4) = (2) - (3)
1981	32.2	11.0	22.2
1982	32.3	10.4	21.9
1983	32.0	10.3	21.7
1984	30.4	10.7	19.7
1985	29.4	9.6	19.8
1986	29.7	8.8	20.9
1987	30.7	8.8	21.9
1988	28.1	8.3	19.8
1989	27.2	8.8	18.4
1990	27.3	8.1	19.2

Source: Sample Registration Survey Reports by the Registrar General of India.

The estimated natural population increase in West Bengal during 1981-91 stands at 21.9%. [This estimate is prepared on the basis of natural population increase in course of a decade, i.e. r_1 r_2. r_{10}, and in accordance with the formula, viz $R = (1+r_1)(1+r_2)(1+r_3) . (1+r_{10}) - 1$.] The estimate of the expert committee on population growth rate was 1.1% below 21.9%, i.e. the rate of natural increase during 1981-91. Nevertheless, the actual population growth rate exceeded the rate of natural population increase by 2.7%, and stood at 24.6% during 1981-91. This increase can largely be accounted for by the influx of people from Bangladesh, Nepal, Bhutan and other regions of India. Thus, the number of migrants / infiltrators to West Bengal during 1981-91 can be calculated at 14,74,000, i.e. 11% of the total population increase of 1,34,00,000. The actual number of outsiders in West Bengal is likely to be much higher, because a very large number of them have presumably escaped detection by Census personnel.

It has been suggested that, during 1971-81 and 1981-91, West Bengal has accommodated 2 million outsiders. Actually, this number should be much larger, because, from Bangladesh alone, 2.95 million Bengali-speaking Hindus have entered into India (mainly West Bengal) during 1974-1991. As Mohiuddin Ahmed, a renowned journalist of Bangladesh, writes: Thus, we encounter a scenario of missing Hindu population in the successive census periods. The extent of this missing population was about 1.22 million during the period of 1974-1981, and about 1.73 million during the last intercensual period 1981-91. As many as 475 Hindus are disappearing every day from the soil of Bangladesh on an average since 1974. How this phenomenon would be interpreted in terms of demography The relevant parameter is obviously migration which provides a clue to the missing link. The following Table illustrates the rise and fall of Hindu and Muslim population in the last fifty year in Bangladesh.

Census Year	Muslims (%)	Hindus(%)
(1)	(2)	(3)
1941	70.3	28.0
1951	76.9	22.8
1961	80.4	18.5
1974	85.4	13.5
1981	86.6	12.1
1991	88.3	10.5

Source: Bangladesh Population Census in 1981 and 91.

It is noteworthy that, of the nearly ten million Hindu refugees leaving East Pakistan for India in course of the 1971 liberation struggle, a large number did not return to Bangladesh. Moreover, of those who returned, a big number, failing to recover movable / immovable properties looted / misappropriated during 1971, came back to India in one or two years. These refugees have not been taken into account by the Bangladesh Census reports. Their number soars above 3 million.

After the successful conclusion of the Bangladesh liberation struggle in 1971, only 2,00,000 out of 1 million stranded non-Bengalis (usually called Biharis) in Bangladesh, could obtain help from International Red Cross Society in order to move over to Pakistan. The Government of Pakistan trumped up a variety of excuses to avoid the repatriation of the other 8,00,000 Biharis, who were compelled to stay on in Bangladesh. As of late 1994 - i.e. after the lapse of 23 years since 1971 - only 2,50,000 Biharis were found to be living amidst subhuman conditions at 66 camps in Bangladesh. Actually, in terms of a natural population increase, the 8,00,000 Biharis should have swelled to more than 1.3 million by 1994. To the question of where have the more than 1 million Biharis vanished from Bangladesh since 1971, the obvious answer is, they have surreptitiously moved into their ancestral places in India (notably in Bihar), and settled down. In one of his recent election utterances, Laloo Prasad Yadav, the Chief Minister of Bihar, has confessed to granting ration cards and voting rights to 100,000 Biharis from Bangladesh. It may be added that some Governments have loudly complained about infiltration of Pakistanis and Bangladeshis into such important cities as Bombay and New Delhi.

In addition, for the 1981-91 period, Bangladesh Census authorities detect the somewhat unique phenomenon of missing population, and estimates the number at 8 million. As already indicated, 1.73 million Hindus are to be included in the figure of 8 million. It is, therefore, entirely plausible that the remainder of 8 million, i.e. 6.27 million Muslims, have infiltrated into various parts of India, notably West Bengal. The Government of Bangladesh naturally observes silence on this vital issue, this silence being occasionally broken by a hackneyed repetition of the announcement that there are no Bangladeshis in India.

DEMOGRAPHICS

Dakshineswar Kali Temple

Tipu Sultan Mosque

St Paul's Cathedral

Languages of West Bengal (2011)

Bengali (86.22%)

Hindi (6.96%)

Santali (2.66%)

Urdu (1.82%)

Nepali (1.27%)

Other (1.07%)

According to the provisional results of the 2011 national census, West Bengal is the fourth-most-populous state in India with a population of 91,347,736 (7.55% of India's population). Bengalis, consisting of Bengali Hindus, Bengali Muslims, Bengali Christians and a few Bengali Buddhists, comprise the majority of the population.

The Marwari, Maithil and Bhojpuri non-Bengali minorities are scattered throughout the state; various indigenous ethnic Buddhist communities such as the Sherpas, Bhutias, Lepchas, Tamangs, Yolmos, and ethnic Tibetans can be found in the Darjeeling Himalayan hill region. Native Magahi speakers are found in Malda district. Surjapuri; a language that is considered to be a mix of Maithili and Bengali, is spoken across northern parts of the state.

The Darjeeling district also has a large Nepali immigrant population, making Nepali a widely spoken language in this region. West Bengal is also home to indigenous tribal Adivasis such as Santhal, Munda, Oraon, Bhumij, Lodha, Kol, and Toto tribe.

There are a small number of ethnic minoritiesprimarily in the state capital, including Chinese, Tamils, Maharashtrians, Odias, Assamese, Malayalis, Gujaratis, Anglo-Indians, Armenians, Jews, Punjabis, and Parsis. India's sole Chinatown is in eastern Kolkata.

As per West Bengal government the official languages are Bengali, Hindi, Kamtapuri, Kurmali, Odia, Punjabi, Rajbanshi, Santali and Urdu. Nepali also has an official status in the three subdivisions of Darjeeling district. As of 2001, in decreasing order of number of speakers, the languages of the state are: Bengali, Hindi, Santali, Urdu, and Nepali.

Religion in West Bengal (2011)

Hinduism (70.54%)

Islam (27.01%)

Christianity (0.72%)

Buddhism (0.31%)

Jainism (0.07%)

Sikhism (0.07%)

Other Religions (1.03%)

Irreligion (0.25%)

West Bengal is religiously diverse, with regional cultural and religious specificities. Although Hindus are the predominant community, the state has a large minority Muslim population. Christians, Buddhists, and others form a minuscule part of the population. As of 2011, Hinduism is the largest religion, with adherents representing 70.54% of the total population, while

Muslims comprise 27.01% of the total population, being the second-largest community as well as the largest minority group. Sikhism, Christianity, Buddhism, and other religions make up the remainder.

Buddhism remains a prominent religion in the Himalayan region of the Darjeeling hills, and almost the entirety of West Bengal's Buddhist population are from this region.

The state contributes 7.8% of India's population. The Hindu population of West Bengal is 64,385,546 while the Muslim population is 24,654,825, as per the 2011 census. The state's 2001–2011 decennial population growth rate was 13.93%, lower than the 1991–2001 growth rate of 17.8%, and also lower than the national rate of 17.64%. The gender ratio is 947 females per 1000 males. As of 2011, West Bengal had a population density of 1,029 inhabitants per square kilometre (2,670/sq mi) making it the second-most densely populated state in India, after Bihar.

The literacy rate is 77.08%, higher than the national rate of 74.04%. Data of 2010–2014 showed the life expectancy in the state was 70.2 years, higher than the national value of 67.9. The proportion of people living below the poverty line in 2013 was 19.98%, declining from 31.8% a decade ago. Scheduled castes and tribes form 28.6% and 5.8% of the population, respectively, in rural areas, and 19.9% and 1.5%, respectively, in urban areas.

In September 2017, West Bengal achieved 100% electrification, after some remote villages in the Sunderbans became the latest to be electrified.

As of September 2017, out of 125 towns and cities in Bengal, 76 have achieved Open Defecation Free (ODF) status. All towns in the districts of Nadia, North 24 Parganas, Hooghly, Burdwan and East Midnapore are ODF zones, with Nadia becoming the first ODF district in the state in April 2015.

A study conducted in three districts of West Bengal found that accessing private health services to treat illness had a catastrophic impact on households. This indicates the importance of public provision of health services to mitigate against poverty and the impact of illness on poor households.

The latest Sample Registration System (SRS) statistical report shows that West Bengal has the lowest fertility rate among Indian states. West Bengal's total fertility rate was 1.6, way below Bihar's 3.4, which is the highest in the entire country. Bengal's TFR of 1.6 roughly equals that of Canada.

RELIGION

Tribals and Hinduism: Some Hindus believe that Indian tribals are close to the romantic ideal of the ancient silvan culture of the Vedic people. Golwalkar said: "The tribals "can be given yajnopavita. They should be given equal rights and footings in the matter of religious rights, in temple worship, in the study of Vedas, and in general, in all our social and religious affairs. This is the only right solution for all the problems of casteism found nowadays in our Hindu society."

At the Lingaraja temple in Bhubaneswar (11th century), there are Brahmin and Badu (tribal) priests. The Badus have the most intimate contact with the deity of the temple, and only they can bathe and adorn it.

There were also tribal reform and rebellion movements during the period of the British Empire, some of which also participated in the Indian freedoom struggle or attacked mission posts. The Bhil tribe is mentioned in the Mahabharata. The Bhil boy Eklavya's teacher was Drona, and he had the honour to be invited to Yudhisthira's Rajasusya Yajna at Indraprastha. Indian tribals were also part of royal armies in the Ramayana and in the Arthasastra.

Bhakta Shabari was a Bhil woman that offered Shri Rama and Shri Laxmana 'ber' when they were searching for Shri Sita in the forest. Maharishi Matanga, a Bhil was became a Brahmana.

Tribal System: Tribal are not part of caste system, This is a eglitarian society. Christian tribals do not automatically lose their traditional tribal rules. When in 1891 a missionary asked 150 Munda Christians to inter-dine with people of different rank, only 20 Christians did so, and many converts lost their new faith.

Father Haghenbeek concluded on this episode that these rules are not "pagan", but a sign of "national sentiment and pride", and wrote: "On the contrary, while proclaiming the equality of all men before God, we now tell them: preserve your race pure, keep your customs, refrain from eating with Lohars (blacksmiths), Turis (bamboo workers) and other people of lower rank. To become good Christians, it (inter-dining) is not required."

9

Art, Architecture, Fair and Festivals

ARTS OF WEST BENGAL

The Indian state of West Bengal has a rich cultural and artistic heritage. Due to the reign of many different rulers in the past, arts and crafts in West Bengal underwent many changes giving an artistic diversity today in the forms of traditional handicrafts, masks, painting and carving, dance, music etc.

Music

The music of West Bengal includes multiple indigenous musical genres such as Baul, Bishnupuri Classical, Kirtan, Shyama Sangeet, Rabindra Sangeet, Nazrul Geeti, Atulprasadi, Dwijendrageeti, Probhati Snageet, Kantageeti, Ganasangeet, Adhunik Gaan, Bengali rock etc. West Bengal has a rich culture with the classical and folk songs.

The Bishnupur Gharana is the sole Classical (*Drupad*) *gharana* of Bengal. It originated in Bishnupur, Bankura by the court musicians of the Malla Kings.The bauls are a mystic group of singers and musicals, immensely popular in the countryside. They perform using a khamak, ektara and dotara. Rabindra Sangeet, also known as Tagore songs, are songs written and composed by Rabindranath Tagore. They have distinctive characteristics in the music of Bengal, popular in India and Bangladesh. Rabindra Sangeet has been an integral part of Bengal culture for over a century. Shyama Sangeet is a genre of Bengali devotional songs dedicated to the Hindu goddess Shyama or Kali which is a form of supreme universal mother-goddess Durga or parvati. It is also known as Shaktagiti or Durgastuti.

Kirtan is also a true song which describe the mythological epic. Chaitanya Mahaprabhu starts the Hare Krishna movement from Nabadwip.

Other songs like Hapu song, Bhadu song, Gombhira, Tusu song, Bhatiyali song, Patua Sangeet etc are the true Bengali folk song, that make the cultural song of West Bengal.

Dance

Dance with Rabindra Sangeet in Kolkata

Dance of West Bengal

Songs and dances are connected with each to each. The rich cultural heritage and creative minds of the people of Bengal are best reflected in their traditional folk dances like *martial dance, harvest dance* etc. In Modern West Bengal rural Bengal takes the lead in keeping the old customs and the associated song and dance. The folk dances of West Bengal deals with a variety of themes. Some are associated with religion, prayers, festivals and rituals, others talk about the society.

Martial Dances

As a cultural tradition there are many Bengali folk dances describing the mythological wars. This martial or war dances are Purulia Chhau dance, Raibenshe dance, Stick dance or Laghur Nritya, Ranapa Dance, Dhali and Paika Nritya, Kukri Nritya etc.

Harvest Dances

The cultural folk dance is mostly related with seasons, sowing of seeds, rains, harvesting in West Bengal. It's celebrated with a lot of ardor by village folks, especially the farming community. Gombhira dance of Malda district is associated with mythology. Tushu dance, Nabanna dance, Nnoila broto etc. are also related with farming. Some tribal dance like Santhali dance, Rabha dance, Mundari dance, Rajbanshi dance etc performed to the accompaniment of a number of musical instrument and are quite elaborated in nature.

Masks

Tribal bamboo mask from Dinajpur

Mask or Mukhosh of West Bengal, as it known has a

mysterious history. Mostly it uses for the Mask Dance, the folk dance of West Bengal. The wearing of these masks is connected with early types of folklore and religion. There is various type of masks made up of clay, wood, sponge wood or shola, pith, paper, metal etc. Generally, half masks are made up of clay, pith and paper and wooden masks are very rare. Some of the masks came from the Tribal of West Bengal. Geographically, West Bengal comes well within this mask using culture zone. Mask in West Bengal is mostly used in folk dance. UNESCO selected The Rural Craft Hub of Bengal to showcase their artwork in Paris in 2015.

Chhau Mask

The most interesting fact, Purulia Chhau Dance is listed on UNESCO's world heritage list of dances. The main difference between the Purulia chhau and Orisha chhau is in the use of the mask. Purulia chhau used the mask in dance, but Orisha does not have the mask thereby adding facial expression with body movement and gesture. Purulia chhau dancer were the earthy and theatrical mask which represent the mythological characters.

Gambhira Mask

Gomira mask is a part of Gomira dance which is originated in North and South Dinajpur of West Bengal. The word *Gomira* is colloquial from *Gram-Chandi*, a female deity. The extract origin of this craft is no doubt very old and some of the craftsmen claim it is at least as old as the beginning of *kaliyug*. The Gomira dances are organized to propitiate the deity to usher in the *good forces* and drive out the *evil forces*. This mask is used in the war dance. It is also called *Mukha Khel* meaning the game of masks.

Others

Ghurni region of Krishnanagar has been a notable center of clay art for a long time. Their clay mask of Durga and the other is well known for their beauty and the mask follow a contemporary style. Kolkata Kumartuli is well-known for clay mask. The masks are made in clay and then sun-dried and finally coloured and decorated with sponge wood or foil. Potter has been receiving a lot of attention for sculpting Bengali deities. Dokra is unique folk art of West Bengal.Metal casting dokra mask is created various contemporary sculptures with this art form. Gita Karmakar, a female artist from Bankura has been awarded the President's award. Her works of Dokra art are equally popular in other countries. Durga face is a well known shola mask of Murshidabad. It's mainly used for the decorate status. For making this masks, shola is pulled from water and dried. Then it is cut with the knife according to the design. The most attractive fact, Murshidabad is recognize for the shola work.

Terracotta Art

Architecture

There are significant examples of fine arts in Bengal from earlier times such as terracotta art of Hindu temples. The roofing style of Bengali Hindu temple architecture is unique and closely related to the paddy roofed traditional building style of rural Bengal.

Terracota Panel of Pratepshbra mandir, Kalna

Roofing styles include the jor-bangla, do-chala, char-chala, at-chala, deul, ek-ratna, pancharatna and navaratna. Bishnupur in West Bengal has a remarkable set of such temples which being built from the Malla dynasty are examples of this style. Most of these temples are covered on the outer surface with terracotta reliefs which contains plenty of secular materials making these important to reconstruct the social structure from these times.

The temple structures contain gabled roofs which are colloquially called the chala, For example, a gabled roof with an eight sided pyramid structured roof with be called "ath chala" or literally the eight faces of the roof. And frequently there is more than one tower in the temple building. These are built of laterite and brick bringing them at the mercy of severe weather conditions of southern Bengal. Dakshineswar Kali Temple is one example of the Bhanja style while the additional small temples of Shivaalong the river bank are example of southern Bengal roof style though in much smaller dimension.

Terracotta dolls

Terracotta or clay craft has been the symbol of man's first attempt at craftsmanship, just as the potter's wheel was the first machine invented to use the power of motion for a productive purpose. However, its association with religious rituals has imbibed it with deeper significance. In West Bengal, terracotta traditions are found from the earliest times. They are symbols of fulfillment of aspirations of village folk. In order to cater to the commercial requirements of the modern global market, the village potter is often combining the traditional rural abstractions with refined urban tastes to show pieces of terracotta art.

Bankura Horse

In Bankura, potters create terracotta horses and elephants. Over the centuries they have moved away from a realistic presentation to a representational presentation. Potter-artists of different regions focused on different parts of the animal body in such a manner that representation of the same became more important than representation of the entire body of the animal.

Manasa chali

Manasa chali is the idol of Debi Manasa. It is an unique terracotta sculpture of Panchmura, West Bengal. Manasa chali has a small figure or a group of three figures in the middle, with rows of snake hoods fanning out in a half moon shape.

Painting

Patachitra

Patachitra painting is a true cultural heritage of West Bengal. The Patua Community of West Bengal has an ancient history to practiced the craft of Patachitra. A quaint little village of Paschim Medinipur, Naya is home to around 250 Patuas or chitrakars. Bengal Patachitra has a various aspect like Chalchitra, Durga Pat, Medinipur Patachitra, kalighat Patachitra, mud wall painting etc. D. P. Ghosh mentioned different style of Bengal Patachitra respecting of the district of West Bengal in his book *Folk Art of Bengal.*

The Patachitra a of different districts of West Bengal are characterized by many peculiarities in colour and design. The patachitra of Manbhum, now known as Purulia can easily be distinguished by their preference for one particular shade of burnt sienna relieved by white and yellow patches and densely packed composition. The seated figures of Dasaratha and Chand Sadagar of Medinipur crowning the Ramayana and Kamale-Kamini scrolls are impressive and monumental. In the scrolls of pot of Birbhum, Bankura and Burdwan preference for Indian red background usually found, the scrolls of Hooghly preferred a dark brown. The Hooghly and Manbhum 'pats' are peculiar and definitely modernistic with the abstract linear treatment.

Chalchitra

Chalchitra is a part of *Bengal Patachitra*, It referred to the *Debi Chal* or *Durga chala*, the background of the Durga Pratima or idol. Patua, the artists of Chalchitra called it as Pata Lekha, means the writing of Patachitra. 300–400 years old idols of Nabadwip Shakta Rash used Chalchitra as a part of Pratima. At a time, the use of Chalchitra became fade, but now it has a great popularity. Chalchitra artist of Nabadwip, Tapan Bhattacharya said-

"It's good to see a lost painting coming back around."

Durga pot

Durga pot or Durga sara is recognised as the worshiped patachitra. It worshiped in the *Hatsarandi Sutradhar society* of Birbhum district on Durga puja time. This type of patachitra is also worshiped is Katwa. Durga Pot has a semi-circular Patachitra where Patachitra of Durga is in the middle position. Ram, Sita, Shib, Nandi-Vringi, Brahma, Vishnu, Shumbha-Nishumbha are painted on this kind of Chalchitra. Krishnanager Rajrajeshwari Durga is seen to be uniquely noticed. In the middle of the Chalchitra, there is Panchanan Shib and Parvati is beside him, on one side there is Dasha-mahabidya and the other side, there is Dashabatar.

Handicrafts

Clay art

Clay art has an indigenous history in West Bengal. Ghurni of Nadia district is very popular for making the clay idols. West Bengal has an ancient heritage of dolls. Dolls have been customarily crafted by women from the potter communities. Dolls made of soft clay and fired-clay are available all over West Bengal. Each of these dolls are made differently. Terracotta dolls of Panchmura, Hingul dolls and Tusu dolls of Bishnupur, Jo dolls of Medinipur, Kanthalia dolls of Murshidabad, Sasthi dolls of Coonoor, Manasha Pot of Dakshindari, Shiva Head of Nabadwip are very famous.

Kantha

Kantha Stitch is one of the most popular handicrafts of Santiniketan in the Birbhum district of West Bengal, India.

Dokra

Dorka art is the most interesting and creative art of West Bengal. The Dokras are now dispersed over the western part of West Bengal in four districts namely Bankura, Purulia, Midnapore and Burdwan and are mainly concentrated in Bankura and partly in Purulia. The Dokra artistes of Bankura make various kinds of images and figurines of gods and goddesses, birds and animals, like Lakshmi, Lakshmi-Narayan, Shiva-Parvati flanked by Ganesh and Kartik, elephants, horses, owls, peacocks etc.

Wooden art

Wooden art is a very old tradition of West Bengal. Wooden protima or idol is seen in Indian Museum. The art-making wooden dolls have been an age-old practice in West Bengal and Natungram is one of them. Natumgram, a village of West Bengal makes wooden dolls like Gouranga, Krishna, Bor-Bou, Gour-Nitai, owl etc. Gomira masks of North and South Dinajpur in West Bengal are also made of wood.

Bamboo craft

Bamboo crafts are a very old and indigenous tradition in West Bengal. Different shapes and patterns of baskets are made using local traditions and techniques. In West Bengal, a tray-like bamboo basket is traditional. Different types of baskets, hand-held fan, sieves etc. are also made and painted with auspicious symbols and are used in marriage and other ceremonies.

ART AND CRAFTS OF WEST BENGAL

West Bengal serves as home to many talented artisans in India. The unique rustic and mystic charm of Bengal crafts is admired by art-lovers the world over. From embroidery to sculpture and sketching to metal crafts, the state has a unique specialization in many forms of craft. The age-old traditional crafts of West Bengal have been so well molded according to the present day demands that it seems that these artisans, apart from their traditional skills, have an expertise in the art of survival as well. Even if you have little understanding of arts and crafts, you will certainly be captivated by the unique handicrafts of West Bengal. Let us know more about them.

Arts & Crafts Of West Bengal

Kantha Embroidery

Kantha is a very beautiful form of embroidery that originated in West Bengal. It is basically the art of outlining decorative images with running stitch, on clothes, with colorful threads. It is used on saris, dhotis, kurtas, ethnic-wear for men and women, bed-linen, cushion covers, quilts and other such items. A craze amongst foreign tourists, Kantha stitch is best used on cotton and silk.

Terracotta Craft

The terracotta craft of West Bengal is famous throughout the world, for its pastoral and rustic charm. The clay-modeled items that form a part of this craft, made with natural colors, are a viewer's delight. They were a craze in Bengal during the reign of Malla rulers, in the 16th-17th century. The temple of Vishnupur stands as marvelous example of the terracotta craft of Bengal.

Scroll Painting

Scroll Painting is done on thick fabrics, with the help of natural colors. Popularly called Pat Chitra in Bengal, they vary in length and height. However an average scroll painting is about 15 ft long. It is divided into a number of compartments, with each compartment carrying an episode of the story being narrated through Pat Chitra.

Conch Shell Crafts

Conch shell craft is one of the most unique and most beautiful forms of handicrafts practiced in West Bengal. It is actually the art of engraving decorative motifs on the natural shells obtained from the ocean. Conchshell crafts are beautiful and delicate, apart from being considered to be extremely auspicious in the Hindu mythology.

Dokra Metal Craft

It is one of the most popular forms of art practiced in Bengal, named after the people who practiced it. It is actually the art of creating statues, jewelries, idols and many other decorative pieces, with the help of clay, wax and molten metal. The best part about Dokra metal crafts is that they are completely original and no replica of any item can ever be made.

Pottery

One of the oldest crafts of Bengal is pottery. It is practiced in the state with beautiful variations, in exquisite styles. Different kinds of pots, like Mangal Ghat, Lakshmi Ghat, Manasha Ghata and Tulsimancha, are designed here. All of them have their own significance and distinctive style. Apart from being practiced for individual purposes, it is also designed and sold on a commercial scale.

Bankura Horses

Bankura horses made from terracotta and considered to be auspicious in West Bengal. They are found adorning one or the other corner, in almost all the Bengali households. They are also used in traditional Bengali rituals, as they are considered to represent the holy horses in Sun God's chariot. When in the state, make sure to buy a sample of this craft, as a souvenir.

Clay Dolls

Putul, as the Bengali dolls are popularly called, are a craze in the European market. Shaped out of clay, painted in vibrant colors and baked in a kiln, they represent the rural Bengal. Out of several varieties of clay dolls in Bengal, the real-life dolls of Krishna Nagar, depicting various social scenes like Collector's court, tea garden, pandit sabha and Charak festival, are the most popular.

Sholapith Craft

Sholapith is a milky-white sponge-wood, used for crafting beautiful decorative pieces. It is also known as 'herbal ivory', as it seems to look like the milky-white items made from ivory. Sholapith is popularly used to craft head-wears of bridal couples, garlands, decorative fans, animals, birds, dolls, Images of gods and Goddesses, elephant-howdahs, peacock-boats, palanquins, flowers various kinds of crowns and backdrop of Durga Pooja stages.

FAIRS AND FESTIVALS IN WEST BENGAL

West Bengal is the state of celebration and varieties. This culturally enriched state has lots to offer to her tourists. There are numerous occasions that make the land, a land of festivals and fairs. Fairs and Festivals of West Bengal are the main attractions when people from different parts of the world come and enjoy. The main feature of the fairs and festivals are that people from various parts of the world come and mish mashes with the true spirit of West Bengal's celebration.

West Bengal makes the people of Indian proud with its wonderful heritage and tradition those are still observed in the form of fairs and festivals. The colorful occasions with a rich mythological background surely impress the tourist coming from various social, religious and economic backgrounds. Without ant economic and religious barrier everyone takes part and make the occasion a grand one.

Fairs and festivals form an inseparable part of the life of people in West Bengal. A Bengali calendar is embellished with celebrations throughout the year, with innumerable festivals for each season. Some of these festivals are celebrated with same passion and devotion throughout the state, while some are confined to a particular zone only, depending upon its mythological or cultural linkage. The festive moods of Bengali people reflect their liveliness and deep-sited belief in their cultural heritage. Let us explore all the major fairs & festivals in West Bengal, in detail.

Basant Utsav

Basant Utsav literally means the 'celebration of spring'. The beautiful tradition of celebrating spring festival in Bengal was first started by Nobel Laureate Rabindranath Tagore, at Vishwabharati Shantiniketan, the University founded by him. Actually,

Bera Utsav

West Bengal is a land of fairs and festivals. In fact, the culture of the state is characterized by the colorful celebrations that adorn it throughout the year. Almost every district of West Bengal plays host to at least one popular fair or festival in the entire year.

Charak Puja

Charak Puja has its own special place in West Bengal, the state of festivals. It is a special folk festival, celebrated for bidding good-bye to the passing year. It is believed that the celebration leads to prosperity in the coming year, wiping out all the sufferings and pains of the current year. This festival is celebrated on the midnight of Chaitra Sankranti,

Durga Pooja

Durga Pooja is the most important festival in West Bengal, celebrated with immense devotion and great pomp and show. This festival is also known by various names here, some call it 'Akalbodhan' - the untimely awakening of Durga, while others refer to it as 'Durgotsab' - the festival of Goddess Durga and even 'Maayer Pujo' - the worship of the Mother Durga.

Ganga Sagar Mela

West Bengal is the state of fairs and festivals. A large number of festivities take place in this state throughout the year. Amongst them, one of the most famous fests is the

Gangasagar Mela. It is held in the month of January-February, on the Ganga Sagar Island, at the mouth of the river Hooghly in Bengal.

Jagaddhatri Puja

The culture of West Bengal is adorned by numerous fairs and festivals. Goddess Durga is one of the most religiously worshipped deities here and many of the festivals celebrated in the state are meant to pay regards to Her only. Jagaddhatri or Jagadhatri puja is one of the festivals observed by the devotees of 'Durga' - the Goddess of Power, who is also called Jagaddhatri i.e. 'the Protector of the World'.

Jalpesh Mela

Jalpesh Mela is an interesting fair in the land of festivals and fairs, West Bengal. It is celebrated in the month of February-March, on the occasion of Shivratri, in Mainaguri town of Jalpaiguri district. It is almost a month-long fair, organized with great pomp and show. Not only the local population, but people from far-flung areas of India also come to participate in this fair.

Jhapan

West Bengal is famous for its rich cultural heritage and the uniqueness of its traditions. There is a festival here for every season and every occasion. Jhapan is one of the most unique festivals celebrated in West Bengal. The festival is dedicated to Goddess Mansha, believed to be the daughter of Lord Shiva, who is also considered to be the Goddess of Snakes.

Kenduli Mela

The people of West Bengal celebrate their cultural lineage with immense love and respect. In fact, the celebration of their art and craft forms an integral part of their cultural heritage. Kenduli Mela is one of those traditional celebrations that celebrate the unique musical art of Baul community, a group of mystic minstrels, in Bengal. This fair is organized in Kenduli city of Birbhum district, the native land of Bauls.

Naba Barsho

Naba Barsho, also known as Poila Baishakh, marks the beginning of New Year in Bengal. It is celebrated on the first day of Baishakh, as per the Hindu calendar. According to the Gregorian calendar, it falls either on April 14 or 15. It is a public holiday in West Bengal, with its celebrations dating back to the reign of Mughal Emperor Akbar. During Akbar's time, the last day of Chaitra (the month before Baishakh) was fixed to be the customary day for clearing all kinds of previous dues.

Poush Mela

West Bengal is the land of fairs and festivals. Innumerable festivals are celebrated throughout the year in the state. Apart from traditional festivals, like Durga Pooja and Diwali, harvest festivals like Jhapan and tourism festival like Teesta Tea and Tourism Festival are observed here. Another festival that Bengali people relish is the 'Cultural Festival of Poush'.

Rash Mela

Colorful festivals and fairs adorn the culture of West Bengal. Hundreds of festivities are held here every year, either to please the myriad deities worshipped by the Bengali people or to celebrate the glory and beauty of something important occurred in the past. Then, there are festivals organized to promote arts, tourism or even celebrate a good harvest.

Rath Yatra

Rath Yatra, which involves taking out of the procession of Lord Jagganath's Chariot, is one of the oldest traditions in Hindu Society. It is celebrated with great effervescence and immense devotion in Orissa and Bengal. Being celebrated since 1397, this Rath Yatra of West Bengal is the second oldest chariot festival in India, after the Rath Yatra of Puri.

Saraswati Puja

Maa Saraswati is the Hindu Goddess of Learning. She is worshipped in almost all the parts of the country with equal devotion. Saraswati Pooja is observed on 'Vasant Panchmi', which falls in the Phalgun month (January-February as per the Gregorian calendar). In almost all the households of West Bengal, Saraswati Pooja is celebrated with immense devotion.

Teesta Tea & Tourism Festival

West Bengal is considered to be the state of festivals .The Bengali calendar is full of fairs and festivals, each of them celebrated for a different reason. There is a festival for every season, every region and every occasion. Each of these festivals has a unique logic behind its celebration.

Vishnupur Festival

Vishnupur, situated in the Bankura district of West Bengal, is the seat of ancient culture of Bengal. Adorned by magnificent art and architecture, this city tells the tale of the golden era of the state. The city of Bishnupur encloses within its boundaries a number of glorious monuments, like Shyam Ray Temple, Jorbangla and Radhey Shyam Temple.

FESTIVALS

There is a famous Bengali saying 'Baro mashe tero parbon' which literally translates as 13 festivals in 12 months. This famous Bengali saying however grossly underestimates the number of festivals, civil and religious, celebrated in Kolkata, where communities belonging to all religions and from all over the subcontinent have brought along their own local cults which even within the Hindu religion vary from area to area.

New Year's Day

The first festival of the year in West Bengal is the New Year's Day. Although most communities follow their own calendar, the first day of the Christian year is celebrated by all. Buses are garlanded. The state is in a festive mood, with decorations from Christmas past still very much in evidence.

As year come to an end the people of West Bengal and get ready to mark the beginning of another year. On the night of

31st December, which is usually chill due to peak winter people forgetting the cold are seen to move around the side walks of Park Street through out the night merry making to glory. On New Year's Eve, parties are organised in clubs, hotels, restaurants and private homes. People go to bed late. Those who manage will go to the races the next day in the afternoon-a hangover 'must' in Kolkata.

Gangasagar Mela

Is the largest fair celebrated in West Bengal. This fair is held where the Ganga and the Bay of Bengal form a nexus. Hence the name Gangasagar Mela.

The river Ganga which originates in the Gangotri glacier in the snow clad Himalayas, descends down the mountains, reaches the plains at Haridwar, flows through ancient pilgrimage sites such as Benares and Prayag, and drains into the Bay of Bengal.

Makar Sankranti

The Makar Sankranti festival which falls in mid-January and marks the winter solstice. During this period pilgrims in numbers more than 500,000 gather on Sagar Dwip, an island some 150 kilometers (93 miles) south of Kolkata, for the three-day Ganga Sagar Mela. The pilgrims on the way to the mela sleeps in make shift tents erected in the Maidan . The festival lasts from 12th to 14th. The Baul Mela beings on the day the Ganga Sagar Mela ends. Bauls are singers belonging to the Hindu Vaishnab and Sufi Muslim from all over Bengal as well as from Bangladesh. They gather at Bolpur which is 150 kilometers (93 miles) west of Kolkata and sings enchanting devotional tunes for three nights.

Saraswati Puja

Late in January or early February, Saraswati Puja, the festival of Goddess of Learning, is celebrated by students, artists and professors. As the winter recedes and spring approaches, the city get ready for the celebration of Vasant Panchami. On this day primarily students, artists and professors offer worship to Devi Swaraswati the Goddess of Knowledge and music.

Dol Purnima

Dol Purnima more popularly known as Holi is a festival of colours and the city celebrates it with the traditional gaiety. Holi is also known as the Dol Yatra in Bengal. It is celebrated by people of all walks of life both young and old by smearing each other with coloured powder especially red. Colours are also mixed with water and sprayed on passer-by. The ever enthusiastic group enjoys by drinking bhang which is a mild-milk beverage laced with marijuana. Social barriers are broken. This is a time when lower-cast plays with the upper-cast and poor may play with the rich.

Noboborsho

Marking the beginning of the Bengali New Year is Noboborsho. It falls on the mid of April the approach of summer. Bengali businessman opens his new account book the halkhata. The account books, statues of Ganesh and Lakshmi is taken to the Temple for blessings. The businessmen invites their loyal customers in the evening who make a token payment to open the new account book. The shops are heavily decorated with floral garlands, young banana and auspicious mango leaves and the customers are greeted with sweets.

A few days after noboborsho, on Mahabir Jayanti, the birth anniversary of last and greatest Jain prophets, there are processions of the Svetamber Sect from Harrison Road to Kalakar Street, and of the Digambar Sect from Belgachaia to Baisakh Lane.

Rath Yatra

The Rath Yatra festival falls on the late of June or early July. It is celebrated in the honour of Lord Jagannath an avatar of Vishnu. Processions are organised in Kolkata by the ISKON and in Serampore, north of Kolkata. People scramble around to get a chance to pull the sacred rope of the huge chariot.

Replicas of Jagannath's chariot are sold at Kalighat. Children decorate their chriots with flowers and place in them clay images of Jagannath, his brother Balaram and sister Subhadra.

Vishwa Karma Puja

Vishwa Karma is the God of Creation. On the 17th. September every year the festival is celebrated by all industrial houses, artists, craftsmen, and weavers. The tools utilized during production are cleaned and all machinery are repainted. The the statue of Vishwakarma holding a hammer are erected in workshops. People are also found to be flying multi-colour kites.

Durga Puja

The start of winter coincides with Durga Puja in October, the most important festival in Bengal. According to Hindu mythology, all gods and goddesses of thee Hindu pantheon endowed Durga with a portion of their own energy to give her strength, or shakti, to destroy the evil forces. Some 2,000 pandals are erected throughout the city. The image of Durga shows her slaying the most powerful demon, Mahisasur.

Laxmi Puja

In the month of October, five days after Mahadashami, on full moon, is the festivals of the Goddess of prosperity Laxmi who is worshipped daily in most Hindu household for the family's well-being. Public Pujas are performed in the same premises as for Durga Puja.

Kali Puja

After nineteen days of the completion of the Durga Puja, the city get geared up to celebrate another popular festival, the Kali Puja. Kali is worshipped as the Mother Goddess who protects from evil. The image of Kali is bit frightening and usually shows her with a severed head in one hand, her sword known as Kharga in the other. She is seen standing on her foot on Lord Shiva's chest and wearing a garland of skulls. The puja actually takes place at midnight on the day of the new moon. During the Kali Puja all houses are lit up with candles decorated around the house. During this puja, children and adults are seen to burst firecrackers and lighting multicouloured sprinkling crackers. No one seems to sleeps on that night.

Kali Puja coincides with Diwali, the North Indian New Year, the festivals of lights. House-holds clean their houses and light up candles all over their houses. Children and adults set off firecrackers all night. No one sleeps on that night.

Two days after that is Brother's Day, Bhai Phonta or Bhatri Dvitiya. Elder sisters dip their little fingers into kajol, a mixture of ghee, rice-paste and almond paste, and put a mark on their brothers' forehead.

Christmas

Christmas is not only celebrated by the Christian community but even other people and communities of Kolkata as well. The famous Park Street is highly illuminated and Flurry bake specials cakes which is sold in no time. Christmas falling during winter which is a very pleasant time of Kolkata, people are seen taking time off to hold picnics. There are parties in clubs and hotels. The best masses are at St. Paul's Cathedral, candle lit on this occasion, at St. Andrew's Kirk.

The Muslim Festivals

Muslim festivals are celebrated with intensity in West Bengal. During Bakrid, marking the end of Ramazan and Id-Ul-Fitr in celebration of the hajis, the pilgrims to the Holy Mecca, the northern part of the Maidan becomes the prayer grounds for Muslims who gather around the Saheed Minar while the muezzin leads the sessions from the top the monument.

The Shiite processions along Chitpore Road and, in Metiaburuz, Kidderpore, Razabazar, Narkeldanga, Beliaghata and Manicktola are really a spectacle to be seen. These procession are led by a white horse, the Hussain's mount. Immediately following are the tazias, preciously handicrafted replicas of Hussain's grave. The flagellants pound their chests singing "Hassan, ya Hussain" and use muti-tailed whip attached with razor flagellate themselves.

Jalpesh Mela (District Jalpaiguri)

On the occasion of Sivaratri (February – March), a month-long fair is held at Jalpesh near Mainaguri in the district of Jalpaiguri. The fair centres round the age-old Siva temple dedicated to Lord Jalpeswara.

Bera Utsav (District Murshidabad)

Every year on the last Thursday of the Bengali month of Bhadra mid-September, Bera Utsav is held at Lalbagh on the river Bhagirathi near the palace of the Nawabs. Fireworks of various size and colour add to the gaiety of the festival.

Jagaddhatri Puja (District Hooghly)

Goddess Jagaddhatri is worshipped in the Bengali month of Kartick (November). At Chandannagar near Kolkata images of the goddess are tall, pandals spectacular and the illumination unique. In fact, the illumination part is the most attractive feature here.

Teesta Tea & Tourism Festival (Inter-State)

Held in a series at Darjeeling, the Dooars and in Sikkim, the Teesta Tea & Tourism Festival is celebrated with a view to promote tourism in this region as a composite tourist destination, with its bounties in tea, timber and tourism. The festival is held every year in November – December.

Vishnupur Festival (District Bankura)

In the temple town of Vishnupur a festival is organised every year between 27 and 31 December. Characterised by exhibition and sale of local handicrafts and performance of the rich musical tradition that Vishnupur boasts, this is an immensely popular festival.

FINE ARTS

Terracotta temple of Bishnupur in Bankura, one of the older examples of the terracotta arts of India

There are significant examples of fine arts in Bengal from earlier times, including the terracotta art of Hindu temples and the Kalighat paintings. Bengal has been in the vanguard of modernism in fine arts. Abanindranath Tagore, called the father of modern Indian art, started the Bengal School of Art, one of whose goals was to promote the development of styles of art outside the European realist tradition that had been taught in art colleges under the British colonial administration. The movement had many adherents, including Gaganendranath Tagore, Ramkinkar Baij, Jamini Roy, and Rabindranath Tagore. After Indian Independence, important groups such as the Calcutta Group and the Society of Contemporary Artists were formed in Bengal and came to dominate the art scene in India.

IMPORTANT FESTIVALS

Durga Puja is the biggest, most popular and widely celebrated festival in West Bengal. The five-day-long colourful Hindu festival witnesses intense celebration across the state. Pandals are erected in various cities, towns and villages throughout West Bengal. The whole city of Kolkata undergoes a transformation during Durga Puja, as it is decked up in lighting decorations and thousands of colourful pandals are set up where effigies of goddess Durga and her four children are worshipped and displayed. The idols of the goddess as brought in from Kumortuli, where idol-makers work round the year fashioning the clay-models of the goddess. Since independence in 1947, Durga Puja has slowly changed into more of a glamorous carnival than a religious festival, where people across diverse religious and ethnic spectrum partake in the festivity. On Vijayadashami, the last day of the festival, the effigies are paraded through the streets with riotous pageantry before being dumped into the rivers.

Rath Yatra is a Hindu festival which celebrates Jagannath, a form of Krishna. It is celebrated with much fanfare in Kolkata as well as in rural Bengal. Images of Jagannath are set upon a chariot and pulled through the streets.

Festivals of West Bengal: Durga Puja, Rath Yatra and Muharram procession in Kolkata.

Other major festivals of West Bengal include Poila Baishakh the Bengali new year, Dolyatra or Holi the festival of lights, Poush Parbon, Kali Puja, Nabadwip Shakta Rash, Saraswati Puja, Deepaboli, Lakshmi Puja, Janmashtami, Jagaddhatri Puja, Vishwakarma Puja, Bhai Phonta, Rakhi Bandhan, Kalpataru Day, Shivratri, Ganesh Chathurthi, Maghotsav, Kartik Puja, Akshay Tritiya, Raas Yatra, Guru Purnima, Annapurna Puja, Charak Puja, Gajan, Buddha Purnima, Christmas, Eid ul-Fitr, Eid ul-Adha, and Muharram. Rabindra Jayanti, Kolkata Book Fair, Kolkata Film Festival, and Nazrul Jayanti are important cultural events.

Eid al-Fitr is the most important festival of Muslims in West Bengal. Muslims celebrate the end of Ramadan with prayers, alms-giving, shopping, gift-giving, and feasting.

Christmas, called *Bô°odin* (Great day) is perhaps the next major festival celebrated in Kolkata, after Durga Puja. Just like Durga Puja, Christmas in Kolkata is an occasion in which all communities and people across religions take part. The state tourism department organises the gala Christmas Festival every year in Park Street. The whole of Park Street is decked out in colourful lights, and food stalls sell cakes, chocolates, Chinese cuisines, momo, and various other items. Musical groups from Darjeeling and other states of North East India are invited by the state to perform choir recitals, carols, and jazz numbers. Buddha Purnima, which marks the birth of Gautama Buddha, is one of the most important Hindu/Buddhist festivals and is celebrated with much gusto in the Darjeeling hills. On this day, processions begin at each of the various Buddhist monasteries, or *gumpas*, and congregate at the Mall, Chowrasta. The Lamas chant mantras and sound their bugles, and students as well as people from all communities carry the holy books or *pustaks* on their heads. Besides Buddha Purnima, Dashain, or Dusshera, Holi, Diwali, Losar, Namsoong or the Lepcha New Year, and Losoong are the other major festivals of the Darjeeling Himalayan region.

Poush mela is a popular winter festival of Shantiniketan, with performances of folk music, Baul songs, dance, and theatre taking place throughout the town.

Ganga Sagar mela coincides with the Makar Sankranti, and hundreds of thousands of Hindu pilgrims converge where the river Ganges meets the sea to bathe en masse during this fervent festival.

10

Education

INTRODUCTION

Extending the system of primary education into tribal areas and reserving places for tribal children in middle and high schools and higher education institutions are central to government policy, but efforts to improve a tribe's educational status have had mixed results.

Recruitment of qualified teachers and determination of the appropriate language of instruction also remain troublesome. Commission after commission on the "language question" has called for instruction, at least at the primary level, in the students' native tongue. In some regions, tribal children entering school must begin by learning the official regional language, often one completely unrelated to their tribal tongue.

Many tribal schools are plagued by high dropout rates. Children attend for the first three to four years of primary school and gain a smattering of knowledge, only to lapse into illiteracy later. Few who enter continue up to the tenth grade; of those who do, few manage to finish high school. Therefore, very few are eligible to attend institutions of higher education, where the high rate of attrition continues. Members of agrarian tribes like the Gonds often are reluctant to send their children to school, needing them, they say, to work in the fields.

On the other hand, in those parts of the northeast where tribes have generally been spared the wholesale onslaught of outsiders, schooling has helped tribal people to secure political and economic benefits. The education system there has provided a corps of highly trained tribal members in the professions and high-ranking administrative posts.

St. Paul's School, Darjeeling, the oldest and highest British public school in Asia

St. Joseph's School, Darjeeling

West Bengal schools are run by the state government or by private organisations, including religious institutions. Instruction is mainly in English or Bengali, though Urdu is also used, especially in Central Kolkata. The secondary schools are affiliated with the Council for the Indian School Certificate Examinations (CISCE), the Central Board for Secondary Education (CBSE), the National Institute of Open School (NIOS), West Bengal Board of Secondary Education or the West Bengal Board of Madrasah Education.

As of 2016 85% of children within the age group of 6 to 17 years attend school (86% do so in urban areas and 84% in rural areas).School attendance is almost universal among the age group of 6 to 14 years, and then drops to 70 percent at the age group 15 to 17 years. There is a gender disparity in school attendance in the age group 6–14 years, more girls than boys are attending school. In Bengal, 71 percent of women aged 15 to 49 years and 81 percent of men aged 15 to 49 years are literate. Only 14 percent of women aged 15 to 49 years in West Bengal have completed 12 or more years of schooling, compared with 22 percent of men. Twenty-two percent of women and 14 percent of men age 15 to 49 years have never been to school. Only 14 percent of women aged 15 to 49 years in West Bengal have completed 12 or more years of schooling, compared with 22% of men.

Some of the notable schools in the city are La Martiniere Calcutta, Calcutta Boys' School, St. James' School (Kolkata), St. Xavier's Collegiate School, and Loreto House, Loreto Convent, Asansol some of which rank amongst the best schools in the country. Many of the schools in Kolkata and Darjeeling are colonial-era establishments housed in buildings that are exemplars of neo-classical architecture. The schools of Darjeeling include St. Paul's, St. Joseph's North Point, Goethals Memorial School, and Dow Hill in Kurseong.

University of Calcutta, the oldest public university of India

West Bengal has eighteen universities. Kolkata has played a pioneering role in the development of the modern education system in India. It was the gateway to the revolution of European education during the British Raj. Sir William Jones established the Asiatic Society in 1794 for promoting oriental studies. People such as Ram Mohan Roy, David Hare, Ishwar Chandra Vidyasagar, Alexander Duff and William Carey played leading roles in the setting up of modern schools and colleges in the city.

The University of Calcutta, the oldest public university in India, has 136 affiliated colleges. Fort William College was established in 1810. The Hindu College was established in 1817. The Lady Brabourne College was established in 1939. The Scottish Church College, which is the oldest Christian liberal arts college in South Asia, started its journey in 1830. In 1855 the Hindu College was renamed the Presidency College. In 2010 it was granted university status by the state government and was renamed Presidency University. Kazi Nazrul University was established in 2012. The University of Calcutta and Jadavpur University are prestigious technical universities. Visva-Bharati University at Santiniketan is a central university and an institution of national importance.

IIT Kharagpur, the first IIT of India

The Auditorium at Indian Institute of Management Calcutta

The front entrance to the academic block of NUJS, Kolkata

Prajna Bhavan, housing the School of Mathematical Sciences and School of RKMVU

Other higher education institutes of importance in West Bengal include St. Xavier's College, Kolkata, Indian Institute of Foreign Trade, Indian Institute of Management Calcutta (the first IIM), Indian Institute of Science Education and Research, Kolkata, Indian Statistical Institute, Indian Institute of Technology Kharagpur (the first IIT), Indian Institute of Engineering Science and Technology, Shibpur (the first IIEST), Indian Institute of Information Technology, Kalyani, National Institute of Technology, Durgapur, National Institute of Technical Teachers' Training and Research, Kolkata, National Institute of Pharmaceutical Education and Research, Kolkata, and West Bengal National University of Juridical Sciences. In 2003 the state government supported the creation of West Bengal University of Technology, West Bengal University of Health Sciences, West Bengal State University, and Gour Banga University.

Jadavpur University (Focus area – Mobile Computing and Communication and Nano-science), and the University of Calcutta (Modern Biology) are among two of the fifteen universities selected under the scheme "University with Potential for Excellence". University of Calcutta(Focus Area –

Electro-Physiological and Neuro-imaging studies including mathematical modeling) has also been selected under the scheme Centre with Potential for Excellence in a Particular Area.

Besides these, the state is home to Kalyani University, The University of Burdwan, Vidyasagar University, and North Bengal University all well as established and nationally renowned to cover education needs at the district level and an Indian Institute of Science Education and Research, Kolkata. Apart from this there is a Deemed university run by the Ramakrishna mission named Ramakrishna Mission Vivekananda University at Belur Math.

There are a number of research institutes in Kolkata. The Indian Association for the Cultivation of Science is the first research institute in Asia. C. V. Raman was awarded the Nobel Prize for his discovery (Raman Effect) done in IACS. The Bose Institute, Saha Institute of Nuclear Physics, S. N. Bose National Centre for Basic Sciences, Indian Institute of Chemical Biology, Central Glass and Ceramic Research Institute, Central Mechanical Engineering Research Institute Durgapur, Central Research Institute for Jute and Allied Fibers, National Institute of Research on Jute and Allied Fibre Technology, Central Inland Fisheries Research Institute, National Institute of Biomedical Genomics (NIBMG), Kalyani, and the Variable Energy Cyclotron Centre are the most prominent.

Notable scholars who were born, worked, or studied in the geographic area of the state include physicists Satyendra Nath Bose, Meghnad Saha, and Jagadish Chandra Bose; chemist Prafulla Chandra Roy; statisticians Prasanta Chandra Mahalanobis and Anil Kumar Gain; physician Upendranath Brahmachari; educator Ashutosh Mukherjee; and Nobel laureates Rabindranath Tagore, C. V. Raman, and Amartya Sen.

MAJOR UNIVERSITIES

University of Kolkata (CU): Formally established on 24 January 1857, the University of Kolkata (also known as Calcutta University) was the first modern university in the Indian subcontinent. It has its main campuses in College Street, Rajabazar, Alipore and a host of affiliated colleges in greater Kolkata.

Formally established on the 24 January 1857, the University of Kolkata (also known as Calcutta University), located in the city of Kolkata (previously Calcutta), India, was the first modern university in the Indian subcontinent. It is a state-government administered urban-based affiliating and research university. It has its main campuses in College Street, Rajabazar, Alipore, Hazra, South Sinthi and a host of affiliated colleges in greater Kolkata.

History: University of Kolkata is the oldest of the modern universities in India. It was founded in 1857 during the administration of Lord Canning (1856–1862), the Governor General of India. Dr. Fredrick John, the education secretary to the then British Government in India, first tendered a proposal to the British Government in London for the establishment of a university in Kolkata, along the lines of London University, but at that time the plan failed to obtain the necessary approval.

However, a proposal to establish two universities, one in Kolkata and the other in Bombay was later accepted in 1854 and the necessary authority was given. The Kolkata University Act came into force on 24 January 1857 and a 41-member Senate was formed as the policy making body of the university. When the university was first established it had a catchment area covering the area from Lahore to Rangoon (now in Myanmar) — the largest of any Indian university.

The first Chancellor and Vice-Chancellor of the Kolkata University were Governor General Lord Canning and Chief Justice of the Supreme Court, Sir James William Colvil, respectively. In 1858, Joddu Nath Bose and Bankim Chandra Chattopadhyay became the first graduates of the university. On 30 January 1858, the Syndicate of the Kolkata University started functioning.

The first meeting of the Senate was held in the Council room of the Kolkata Medical College. A temporary office of the university was started in a few rented rooms in Camac Street. For several years afterwards the meetings of the Senate and Syndicate were held in a room of the Writers' building. 244 candidates appeared for the first Entrance Examination of the university, held in March 1857 in the Town Hall of Kolkata. In 1862, a decision was taken by the Senate to construct for the university a building of its own. Accordingly, the historical Senate Hall was constructed at a cost of Rs. 2,52,221/- and inaugurated on 12 March 1873 by holding the convocation of the university.

In 1875 Mohindra College, Patiala in Punjab province of British India became one of the first colleges to be affiliated with University of Kolkata. Later many institutions came under its jurisdiction. Kadambini Ganguly and Chandramukhi Basu became the first lady graduates of the country in 1882. The Hon'ble Justice Gooroodas Banerjee became the first Indian Vice-Chancellor of University of Kolkata in the year 1890. Sir Ashutosh Mukherjee was the Vice-Chancellor for four consecutive two-year terms (1906-1914) and a fifth two-year term (1921–23).

Tradition and Continuity

Modelled on the University of London, the University of Calcutta's current courses include:

- agriculture
- arts,
- commerce,
- social welfare,
- business management,
- education,
- journalism,
- library science,
- engineering,
- technology,
- fine arts,
- music,

- home science,
- law,
- science,
- information technology,
- women's studies,
- forensic science,
- sports,
- mass communication,
- counselling.

At a Glance

Kolkata University currently has:

- 58 departments,
- 18 research centres,
- 650 teachers,
- 3000 non-teaching staff and
- 12,400 post-graduate students.

A Tradition of Notable Firsts

- The first university located to the east of Suez to teach European Classics, English Literature, European and Indian Philosophy and Occidental and Oriental History.
- The first medical school of Asia, the Kolkata Medical College was set up in 1835. Later it was affiliated to the university.
- The first college for women in India, the Bethune College was set up in 1879.
- The nation's first homeopathy college was established in 1880.
- The Science College was established in 1917, the first in India.
- The first blind school in India came into being in 1925.
- The first university museum in India, The Ashutosh Museum, came into being in 1937.

- The Government Arts College was established in 1951.
- The Indian Institute of Social Welfare and Business Management (IISWBM) was set up in 1953 as the country's first management institute.

Academic Milieu

Students from the university have been taking higher studies abroad since its inception. Its alumni are to be found all over the world. During the British era and in the era after Independence to the 1980s, the preferred destinations for pursuing advanced studies were primarily the United Kingdom, United States of America, Eire, France, Soviet Union and Germany.

Recent preferences for visiting students of this university include, apart from the above, Canada, Australia, New Zealand, the Commonwealth of Independent States, Cyprus, China, Japan, Hong Kong, and Singapore.

Also, in a contrast to the previous era, where the preferred subjects were Humanities, Science, Engineering, Medicine, and Law, the currently preferred subjects are:

- Business Management,
- Finance,
- Commerce,
- Communication,
- Information Technology,
- Fashion Designing,
- Hospitality Management,
- Biotechnology,
- Genetics,
- Robotics, and
- Nanotechnology.

Recent surveys among students also indicate an increasing demand for subjects that relate to natural sciences, humanities and social sciences.

Departments/Sections:

- Department of English, University of Kolkata
- Department of Law Kolkata University
- Department of Applied Physics, University of Kolkata
- A. K. Choudhury School Of Information Technology, University of Kolkata
- Department of Statistics, University of Kolkata

Recent accreditation and recognition:

- NAAC Five Star Recognition

The university was awarded the 'five star university' status by the National Assessment and Accreditation Council in 2001.

- Ranking of Institute of Higher Education, Shanghai Jiao Tong University, China

The Institute of Higher Education, Shanghai Jiao Tong University, China recently prepared a list of the world's top 500 institutions of higher learning (universities, research institutes, etc.). The complete list is now available on the internet under the heading "Academic Ranking of World Universities, 2004". The University of Kolkata was the only multi-disciplinary university from India to appear on the list. The other institutions from India on the list, for that year, were the Indian Institute of Science, Bangalore and the Indian Institute of Technology, Kharagpur.

- CU gets "Potential for Excellence" tag of University Grants Commission

On December 8, 2005, the Indian University Grants Commission declared Kolkata University as a "University with Potential for Excellence".

- The world's top arts and humanities universities

On November 10, 2005, The Times Higher Education Supplement published its list of the world's top arts and humanities universities. CU, ranked 39, was the only Indian university to make it to the top 50 list in that year.

Notable Alumni/faculty

Three Nobel Laureates:

- Rabindranath Tagore,
- Sir Chandrasekhara Venkata Raman and
- Amartya Sen,

One Academy Honorary Award winner Satyajit Ray was associated with this University as were two past Presidents of India:

- Dr. Rajendra Prasad and
- Dr. Sarvepalli Radhakrishnan.

Netaji Subhas Chandra Bose, Head of State and Prime Minister of Arzi Hukumate Azad Hind (1942-1945) and co-founder of the Indian National Army was an alumnus.

Other important political leaders of South Asia who were its alumni include:

- Jagjivan Ram, former Deputy Prime Minister of India
- Dr. Anugrah Narayan Sinha,brilliant student and alumni,later first finance minister of Bihar.
- Dr. Ba Maw, who in 1937, became the first Burmese premier under British rule and was head of state in the first sovereign (although pro-Japanese) government during World War II (August 1943-May 1945),
- Muhammad Ali Bogra and
- Huseyn Shaheed Suhrawardy, both of them being former Prime Ministers of Pakistan
- Abdus Sattar, former President of Bangladesh
- Bishweshwar Prasad Koirala, former Prime Minister and senior politician of Nepal
- Romanian-American religious scholar and philosopher Mircea Eliade studied at the University in the late 1920s and early 1930s.
- In 1883 Kadambini Ganguly (nee Basu) and Chandramukhi Basu became the first women graduates

from the University. In the process, they became the first female graduates of the British Empire.

- Kadambini Ganguly also went on to be the first lady physician to be trained in the European system of medicine in South Asia. In 1886, she received her medical degree from the University.
- Chandramukhi Basu later became the principal of Bethune College, thus becoming the first female administrator of an undergraduate academic institution in South Asia.
- Kamini Roy, first female honours graduate in the British Empire, first feminist author in India
- Upendranath Brahmachari, renowned physician and nominee for the Nobel prize in 1929 in the category of physiology and medicine
- Binay Ranjan Sen, former ambassador of India to the USA, Italy and Yugoslavia, Japan, and Mexico and former Director General, Food and Agriculture Organization, UNO
- Satyabrata Rai Chowdhuri, renowned political scientist, emeritus professor, fellow of London University and a former Oxford don of international affairs
- Suniti Kumar Chatterjee - brilliant student and alumni, later National Professor.
- Gayatri Chakravorty Spivak, a noted deconstructionist, feminist, and translator.
- Subimal Sinharoy Indian geologist

Important writers include:

- Rabindranath Tagore
- Benjamin Walker
- Jadavpur University (JU)

Jadavpur University (JU) is a premier educational and research institution in India.

It is located in Kolkata, West Bengal and comprises two campuses — the main campus at Jadavpur and the new campus at Salt Lake. Four specialized institutes are affiliated to Jadavpur University are Jadavpur Vidyapith College of Education, Institute of Business Management, Shrimati J. D. Birla Institute, Marine Engineering and Research Institute.

Jadavpur University is also closely affiliated to leading research institutes like the Indian Association for the Cultivation of Science and the Central Glass and Ceramics Research Institute.

Jadavpur University

Jadavpur University (JU) is a state-funded university and a premier educational and research institution in India. It is located in Kolkata, West Bengal and comprises two campuses - the main campus at Jadavpur and the new campus at Bidhan Nagar (Salt Lake). Jadavpur University is closely affiliated to leading research institutes like the Indian Association for the Cultivation of Science and the Central Glass and Ceramics Research Institute.

History: The National Council of Education (NCE) was set up in 1906 to impart literary, scientific and technical education on a national basis. The year was significant in Bengal's history as the province had just been partitioned by Lord Curzon, the Governor-General of India, into East Bengal on the one hand (the area that was eventually to become Bangladesh in 1971) and West Bengal and Orissa on the other.

This was an extremely unpopular move by the British and was ultimately reversed in 1911, but much damage had been done to Bengal's sensibilities in the meantime. In 1906, a group of Bengali intellectuals including Rabindranath Tagore, Aurobindo Ghosh, Raja Subodh Chandra Mullick and Brajendra Kishore Roychowdhury decided that they would protest the partition of Bengal by setting up an institution that would challenge British rule by offering education to the masses 'on national lines and under national control'. The NCE was set up with Rash Behari Ghosh as its first president.

Virtually at the same time, a rival organisation, the Society for Promotion of Technical Education in Bengal, was set up by

Taraknath Palit, and under it the Bengal Technical Institute came into being on 25 July 1906. The two organisations fought it out for a few years until the SPTE was amalgamated with the NCE in 1910 and the Bengal Technical Institute passed into its hands. In 1921 the Institute became the first in India to introduce Chemical Engineering as a discipline.

By 1940, the institute was virtually functioning as an independent university, and after Indian Independence in 1947, the West Bengal State Legislature, with the concurrence of the Government of India, enacted the Jadavpur University Act, 1955 to convert the institute into Jadavpur University with full autonomy on (December 24, 1955). Since then the university has observed this date in its calendar as Convocation Day.

The emblem of Jadavpur University was designed by the Bengal Renaissance artist Nandalal Bose. As the university celebrated its Golden Jubilee on December 24, 2005, a special emblem (see above) was created to commemorate the occasion. This date was also the centenary of the National Council of Education.

Organization: Jadavpur University is home to over 5000 undergraduate and over 4000 graduate students. It comprises three faculties:

- Faculty of Engineering and Technology
- Faculty of Science
- Faculty Of Arts

It hosts 34 departments under these three faculties besides 16 interdisciplinary schools and 21 research centres. Admission to the Engineering faculty departments is on the basis of a Joint Entrance Examination (WB-JEE) conducted by Government of West Bengal that can be taken by all Indian nationals. Lateral admission through other entrance examinations have also started from 2005.

Each faculty is headed by a Dean, performing administrative and academic duties under principles formulated by the Faculty Councils, while the constituent departments are under the administrative control of respective Heads of the Departments, who function under the policies framed by the Boards of Studies.

The Vice-Chancellor is the chief academic and administrative officer of the university, and is elected from amongst the professors for fixed terms. The Governor of the state of West Bengal is the ex-officio Chancellor of the University, and as such wields no administrative power. Each department offers under-graduate and/or post-graduate programmes, and undertakes research in their respective fields of study.

Four specialized institutes are affiliated to Jadavpur University:

- Jadavpur Vidyapith College of Education - an affiliated high school
- Institute of Business Management - an affiliated business school
- Shrimati J. D. Birla Institute - an affiliated women's college
- Marine Engineering and Research Institute - an independent affiliated research institute, entrance to which is through the prestigious IIT-JEE entrance examinations

Special Areas of Research and Advanced Studies: The University specialises in Oceanography, Electronics & Telecommunication, Computer Science & Engineering, Mechanical Engineering, and Electrical Engineering. It is also one of the only three institutions in eastern India which offers courses and undertakes research in Architecture and Planning. The university has a number of departments recognised by the University Grants Commission (UGC) as Centres for Advanced Study in their respective disciplines, notably English, Comparative Literature and Philosophy.

In collaboration with the Indian Statistical Institute, the university developed the ISIJU, India's first indigenously made transistor-driven computer, in 1966.

This was at the frontier of the technology then available and in recognition the UGC sanctioned a computer centre at part of the electronics department, one of the earliest in the country. In 1988, this finally became an independent department.

The university has received several major grants in recent times to develop new areas and technologies such as cognitive science and mobile computing. Other areas of emphasis include nanotechnology, archives and records, media and communication, and history of the book.

The School of Cultural Texts and Records, started by Professor Sukanta Chaudhuri has been archiving the papers, memoirs and manuscripts of various noteworthy literatures such as Sudhindranath Datta, the editor of the early twentieth century periodical *Parichaya*, and Buddhadeb Bosu, a noted Bengali poet, and will be creating digital archives of many important cultural and historical documents. It is also building an archive of early recorded classical Hindustani music. The project is being undertaken by Professor Amlan Das Gupta.

The university has one of the earliest (1989) schools of women's studies in an Indian university, which has recently introduced an M.Phil programme.

The university also houses the eastern regional centre of the National Afforestation and Eco-Development Board of India.

Recognition and Endowments: Jadavpur University has been formally recognized as a leading university in the past decade by the University Grants Commission (UGC) and the National Assessment and Accreditation Council (NAAC) which have evaluated the university to be in top bracket of accredited Indian educational institutions. The university was the first Indian university to be endowed with the million dollar grant from the Ryoichi Sasakawa Young Leaders Fellowship Fund (SYLFF) under the Nippon Foundation, Japan in 2003.

Notable past/present faculty:

- Amartya Sen (Economics) - Previously Master of Trinity College, Cambridge & The Bank of Sweden Prize in Economic Sciences in Memory of Alfred Nobel awardee

- Buddhadeb Bosu (Comparative Literature) - Author, Sahitya Akademi award winner and Padma Bhushan awardee
- Alokeranjan Dasgupta (Comparative Literature) - Poet, Goethe Medal winner & Sahitya Akademi award winner
- Shankha Ghosh (Bengali) - Poet laureate & Sahitya Akademi award winner
- Nabaneeta Dev Sen (Comparative Literature) - Author & Padma Shree awardee
- Paritosh Sen - Leading Indian artist

Distinguished alumni:

- Satyabrata Rai Chowdhuri - eminent political scientist and author, fellow of the University of London
- Swadesh Chatterjee (Instrumentation Engineering) - President, IAFPE & Padma Bhushan awardee
- Rituparno Ghosh (Economics) - Film director and National Award winner
- Asoke K. Laha (Electronics & Telecommunications) - Founder and Vice-President, Interra IT
- Bhaskar Chaudhuri (Pharmacy) - CEO, Dow Pharmaceutical Sciences, USA
- Moon Moon Sen (Comparative Literature) - Actor in Bengali and Hindi films.
- Nayan Chanda (History) - noted editor and journalist, recipient of the *Shorenstein Award* for Journalism

TRANSITION PROCESS OF EDUCATION

In West Bengal Education system in West Bengal has gone through a drastic change to provide quality education to every student. Authorities have enforced the rule of 'aggregate marking' technique to measure student's level of knowledge. State government has also taken steps to provide special tutorial classes to civil service students. These new ideas have increased momentum of development, which is proceeding to give a new facelift to the education system.

Primary Education- West Bengal primary education is the

first stage of training a student to step into the world of competition. There are more than 67926 schools in West Bengal. Government of West Bengal understands that education is more than just printed alphabets on books. That's why they try their best to educate students with practical approach.

Secondary Education- Secondary schools in this state are under direct authority of Central board of secondary education (CBSC), Indian certificate of Secondary Education (ICSE) and West Bengal board of secondary education (WBSC). West Bengal has become a leader in developing education infrastructure in India by making education available to all. Guidance of skilled and experienced teachers help the students to have a solid educational foundation, which helps them to do great in their higher studies.

College Education- Number of colleges in West Bengal has already exceeded 260 and still growing in number. West Bengal is particularly known for its tremendous capability of providing higher education with the help of Engineering colleges, B.Ed colleges, commerce colleges and all the important education streams. The colleges of arts and science have always shown their competence in producing scholars and leaders. In addition, the affinity of modern people towards fashion and business management courses has compelled the state government to establish new institutions of fashion designing and management in Kolkata and other places of West Bengal.

Universities- Universities of West Bengal offer Undergraduate, Doctoral, Post Graduate, Diploma and Certificate programs. Every course is unique in design and proficiency. While coping with the modernization of education, these universities offer traditional distance learning programs. Currently, there are 22 universities in West Bengal. Most of them are state governed.

Bibliography

Agarwal, Beena : *The Plays of Rabindra Nath Tagore : A Thematic Study*, New Delhi, Satyam Pub., 2003.

Alva, Joachim: *Leaders of India,* Bombay, Thacker & Co., Ltd., 1943

Andrews, C.F. : *Rabindranath Tagore : Selected Stories*, New Delhi, Srishti, 2004.

Anthony, J. Parel : *Hind Swaraj or Indian Home Rule*, Cambridge University Press, 1925.

Arabinda Poddar : *Mamata: The Political Personality*, Kolkata, Indiana, 2004.

Austin, Granville: *The Indian Constitution: Cornerstone of a Nation*, Oxford, Clarendon Press, 1966.

Aziz, K. K.: *Complete Works of Mamata*, Islamabad, National Commission on Historical and Cultural Research, 1978.

Bhattacharya, Sabyasachi : *Vande Mataram : The Biography of a Song*, New Delhi, Penguin, 2003.

Chaudhuri, Sukanta : *Rabindranath Tagore : Selected Writings for Children*, New Delhi, Oxford University Press, 2002.

Fernandes, Vivian: *Modi: Leadership, governance and Performance.* Orient Publishing. Delhi, 2014

Gaur, Sanjay: *Narendra Modi : Change We can Believe In*, Yking Books, Delhi, 2014.

Ghose, S.K.: *Politics of Violence: Dawn of a Dangerous Era*, Springfield, Nataraj, 1992.

Gurumurthy, S. : *Hindu Heritage, Assimilative, Not Divisive*, Vigil, Madras 1993.

Heyman, Michael : *The Tenth Rasa : An Anthology of Indian Nonsense*, New Delhi, Penguin, 2007.

Hoffman, Bruce: *Inside Terrorism*, New York: Columbia University Press, 1998.

Hussein, Abdullah : *Downfall by Degrees,* New Delhi, Katha, 2004.

Ira Mervin Lapidus, *Muslim Cities in the Later Middle Ages,* Cambridge, Mass, 1967.

Kalindi Randeri: *Narendra Modi : The Architect of A Modern State,* Rupa, Delhi, 2009.

Knipe, M.: *Hinduism: Experiments in the Sacred*, Harper, San Francisco, 1991.

Maheshwari, Shriram: *Rural Development in India: A Public Policy Approach*, New Delhi, Sage, 1995.

Mukherjee, Aparna : *The Social Philosophy of Rabindranath Tagore,* New Delhi, Classical, 2004.

Narula, Sanjay : *Mamata and Indian Politics*, New Delhi, Murari Lal and Sons, 2007.

Neale, Walter C.: *Economic Change in Rural India: Land Tenure and Reform in the United Provinces, 1800-1955*, New Haven, 1962.

Nigamananda Das : *Ecology, Myth and Mystery : Contemporary Poetry in English from Northeast India,* New Delhi, Sarup and Sons, 2007.

Pal, Adesh, Anupam Nagar and Tapas Chakraborty : *Decolonisation : A Search for Alternatives*, New Delhi, Creative, 2001.

Prithwis Chandra : *Descriptive Bi-Lingual Catalogue of Chinese Books : In the Collection of the Asiatic Society*, Calcutta, Calcutta, Asiatic Society, 2000.

Richards, J. F. : *The Mughal Empire*, New York: Cambridge University Press, 1993.

Roy, Pabitrakumar : *Rabindranath Tagore,* New Delhi, Munshiram Manoharlal, 2002.

Sardesai, Rajdeep: *2014: The Election That Changed India,* Delhi, 2014.

Talageri, Shrikant : *Aryan Invasion Theory and Indian Nationalism,* Voice of India, Delhi, 1993.

Wilbur L.Cross : *The Development of the English Novel*, New Delhi, Atlantic, 2001.

Yadav, Kripal Chandra : *India's Unequal Citizens : A Study of Other Backward Classes,* Manohar, New Delhi, 1994.

Yasin, Mohammad : *Indian Politics : Processes, Issues and Trends,* New Delhi, Kanishka, 2004.

Zaidi, A. Moin: *Evolution of Muslim Political Thought in India,* New Delhi: S. Chand, 1975.

Index

H

I

J

L

M

N

P

R

S

T

W

❑❑❑

www.ingramcontent.com/pod-product-compliance
Ingram Content Group UK Ltd.
Pitfield, Milton Keynes, MK11 3LW, UK
UKHW042016290726
14061UKWH00001BB/19